# AT KNIT'S END

# At Knit's End

*Meditations for Women Who
Knit Too Much*

STEPHANIE PEARL-McPHEE

Storey Publishing

*The mission of Storey Publishing is to serve our customers by publishing practical information that encourages personal independence in harmony with the environment.*

Edited by Siobhan Dunn and Deborah Balmuth
Cover design by Kent Lew
Cover illustration © Kent Lew
Text design and production by Jennifer Jepson Smith

   For additional information, please contact Storey Publishing, 210 MASS MoCA Way, North Adams, MA 01247.
   Storey books are available for special premium and promotional uses and for customized editions. For further information, please call (800) 793-9396.

Printed in the United States by Versa Press
10 9 8 7 6 5 4

Library of Congress Cataloging-in-Publication Data

Pearl-McPhee, Stephanie.
   At knit's end : meditations for women who knit too much / Stephanie Pearl-McPhee.
      p. cm.
   ISBN 13: 978-1-58017-589-0
   ISBN 10: 1-58017-589-9 (alk. paper)
   1. Knitting—Quotations, maxims, etc. 2. Knitters (Persons)—Quotations. 3. Knitting—Humor. I. Title.
TT820.P373 2005
746.43'2—dc22

                                          2005004007

*For Joe, Amanda, Megan, and Samantha,*
*who have never said one word about all*
*the yarn. I love them to distraction.*

# The Path to Knit's End

In High Park, near my home in Toronto, there is a paved circle with a complex path painted on it, completely surrounded by trees and gardens. Grenadier Pond sits to one side and an elaborate castle playground is nearby. I have walked by it many, many times and my children have always played on it, leaping from one path to another, running the fancy route laid out by the faded painted markings.

When I was finishing this book and had only the introduction to write, I walked through High Park, taking my usual peaceful path through the trees. I was a little angry with myself. I was almost done with the book, and I liked it. Writing the intro at the end seemed silly and redundant, and I was frustrated that I hadn't had the good sense to write it at the beginning when I should have. Writing the intro at the end was a critical error, like knitting the collar of a sweater first, then trying to make all the other pieces fit. How could I possibly go backward to the introduction?

I walked by the paved circle and absentmindedly looked over at it. An elderly lady stood outside the circle. She bowed, then deliberately walked the path marked on the circle. I noticed then that the circle was not a maze, as I had thought. It was instead a looped circular path to the center; there were no wrong turns, there was no chance for confusion. She followed the markings to the exact middle of the circle, and she stood there. I waited. What was she doing? She bowed four times, once in each of the four directions, then peacefully and purposefully retraced her steps back out of the circle. She bowed deeply then, and walked into the woods. I was astonished. She had used this circle in a way that my children and I hadn't imagined. What was a playground to us was clearly a spiritual experience to her.

I walked to the circle and looked around me. A sign that I had never noticed stood nearby. It announced that this was a labyrinth. One walked the route laid out on it, and its quiet, perfect path afforded a chance for spiritual reflection and meditation.

I felt horrible. I had let my children run on it. Here was this incredible, deep, meaningful thing and my children had tramped all over it, laughing and screaming like it was a common plaything. I was mortified. I mentally tried to count how many times we had defiled the thing. Had people who were there to use it for its intended purpose seen us? Were they offended? I turned into the woods to walk home.

That's when it hit me. The labyrinth was like knitting. It was like the book. It was my intro done backward. There was no wrong way to use it. It was all right for the kids to run on it; it didn't have to be a meditative experience for them. Like knitting, it was okay for everyone to have his or her own experience of the thing. It could be a powerful, spirit-moving experience that gave you a better sense of self, it could be a creative outlet, or it could just be fun, or funny.

There's a lot of humor in knitting, though I know you wouldn't think it to see yarn just sitting there. No matter how it is for you, it is enough that knitting is just there . . . like the labyrinth. We can each use it in our own way. So take this book and your knitting and do your thing. There are no wrong answers; there is no right way. We are all knitters.

*There is a certain majesty in simplicity which is far above all the quaintness of wit.*
— ALEXANDER POPE

It is some kind of miracle that all knitting is constructed of only two stitches: knit and purl. Sure, you throw in some yarn overs, and sometimes you knit the stitches out of order, but when it really comes down to it, knitting is simplicity. The most incredible gossamer lace shawl . . . the trickiest aran . . . a humble sock . . . each just made with knit and purl.

*Know these two stitches; Rule the world.*

*Fate laughs at probabilities.*
— EUGENE ARAM

The chances of running out of yarn on a project are directly related to the difficulty that you will have getting more. For example, if you purchased the yarn for a dollar at your local yarn shop, and the owner has set aside an extra 10 balls for you, you are going to have plenty, even without going back. If, however, you purchased the yarn in Italy on a once-in-a-lifetime trip and it was very expensive, you are absolutely going to run out, regardless of careful planning.

*I will always buy extra yarn. I will not try to tempt fate.*

# Knitting:

*construction of a fabric made of interlocking loops of yarn by means of needles.*

— The Columbia Encyclopedia,
Sixth Edition, 2001

Sounds simple enough, doesn't it?

*I will resist the urge to underestimate the complexity of knitting.*

*No, it wasn't an accident, I didn't say that.*
*It was carefully planned, down to the tiniest*
*mechanical and emotional detail.*
*But it was a mistake.*
— NEVIL SHUTE

Everyone has one — a knitting monstrosity. It is not a surprise to me that everybody has one of those "What was I thinking" sweaters, because I have several. What is a surprise is how long the knitter must have ignored the writing on the wall. To get a finished monstrosity, hours and hours of patient denial must be put in. It is a knitter's unfailing and remarkable ability to believe, even when something begins to look monstrous, and keeps looking that way through all the knitting, that somehow it can overcome anything and will be beautiful in the end . . . that is the real surprise.

*Not every project is meant to be.*

*What we love to do we find time to do.*
— JOHN L. SPALDING

Everybody tells me that they would love to knit, but they don't have time. I look at people's lives and I can see opportunity and time for knitting all over the place. The time spent riding the bus each day? That's a pair of socks over a month. Waiting in line? Mittens. Watching TV? Buckets of wasted time that could be an exquisite lace shawl. Eating, sleeping, and laundry? Sweaters.

*There is practically no activity that cannot be enhanced or replaced by knitting, if you really want to get obsessive about it.*

*I just thought of something funny . . .*
*your mother.*
— CHEECH MARIN

There is absolutely no escaping it. The daughters who once thought me clever, beautiful, and fun-loving have finally reached an age where they care about what their mother is doing in public. They ask me if I really need to wear "that" or if I could try not to speak to their friends. They have concerns about the way I laugh and my "dorky" shoes. The worst thing, worse even than the coffee spilled on my jeans or the way I forgot my lipstick again, the proof that I care nothing for their social standing is the knitting.

"Mother," my 15-year-old groans as I take out my sock at the concert. "Could you pretend to be normal?"

*I will continue to freak out my children by knitting in public. It's good for them.*

*I love deadlines. I especially love the whooshing sound they make as they fly by.*
— Douglas Adams

It is a peculiarity of knitters that they chronically underestimate the amount of time that it takes to knit something. Birthday on Saturday? No problem. Socks are small. Never mind that the average sock knit out of sock-weight yarn contains about 17,000 stitches. Never mind that you need two of them. (That's 34,000 stitches, for anybody keeping track.)

Socks are only physically small. By stitch count, they are immense.

*When confronted with a birthday in a week I will remember that a book can be a really good present, too.*

*Any activity becomes creative when the doer cares about doing it right, or doing it better.*
— JOHN UPDIKE

Looking at the work in the gallery I am quietly astonished. The work is so beautiful that I am stunned into standing quietly in front of it for some time. It is a wall hanging by knitter Debbie New, and it depicts the Madonna and Child. It is not knitted in rows, but in a breathtaking spiral freeform technique. The colors and textures of her yarn are applied in a way that makes oil paints look limiting. Debbie New's work answers the question "Is knitting art or craft?" Standing in front of it, with my lowly sock project in my pocket, I am torn between striving to elevate my own work and dropping it into a trash can on the way out.

*Knitting is a unique practice in that its artistic value rests only in its application.*

*Not all who wander are lost.*
— J. R. R. TOLKIEN

It is a little known fact that much like birds, who can always find north, knitters can always find yarn. They can often be found seemingly wandering a store, with no clear goal, driven only by the vague feeling that there is something good nearby. Similarly, when driving through a town that they have never been in, they are often moved by forces unknown to stop for coffee or a restroom break eerily close to the only yarn shop for a hundred miles.

*Respect your inner compass. It points to yarn.*

*If necessity is the mother of invention, then resourcefulness is the father.*
— BEULAH LOUISE HENRY

I am pretty darned sure that knitting with wire was not a knitter's intentional artistic act, but instead the desperate move of an obsessive knitter trapped in a town with no yarn shop . . . but five hardware stores.

*I will not allow my creative spirit and need to knit to be thwarted by a lack of materials.*

*It is the working man who is the happy man.*
*It is the idle man who is the miserable man.*
— BENJAMIN FRANKLIN

My daughter and I were trapped in a seemingly endless bank line. Now me, I'm an experienced mother. I had a children's book, a baggie of snacks, and my knitting in my purse. I've been in this line before and now I come prepared. The woman in line ahead of us had come with nothing but her son and her wits, and she was showing clear signs of not only losing her temper but also developing a twitch over one eye. My daughter watched the woman become increasingly agitated and finally commented to the woman's son, "Your mom should get some knitting; that's what my mommy looks like without it."

*I recognize that knitting can improve my mood in trying circumstances.*

*To invent, you need a good imagination
and a pile of junk.*
— THOMAS A. EDISON

The colors, textures, and quantities available in one's stash are the knitter's pile of junk for inventing. As with all inventing, you can expect it to end badly from time to time. With knitting, there are no explosions or clouds of noxious gasses, there's just some kid opening a box from his Auntie Mary and seeing an orange and puce sweater with a ruffled V-neck, three-quarter-length sleeves, and really clever cables.

*Birthdays are not always the best time to introduce experimental inventions.*

*Any man who afflicts the human race*
*with ideas must be prepared to see them*
*misunderstood.*
— H. L. MENCKEN

Some time ago, I designed a sweater. It was knit of the softest wool, in a color that was perfection itself. The subtle heathered yarn was a soft forest green that would have been perfect had I chosen to hide in a bed of creeping thyme. To me, it was breathtaking. My friend admired my sweater and asked for my pattern. Imagine my shock when several months later she proudly showed me her version, knit dizzyingly from a shiny variegated acrylic yarn that would have been perfect for hiding in a disco. She loved it, and I hoped she wouldn't tell anyone that it was my pattern.

*I will acknowledge that what happens to my patterns after they leave me is none of my business.*

*Insanity in individuals is something rare —*
*but in groups, parties, nations, and epochs,*
*it is the rule.*

— FRIEDRICH NIETZSCHE

A knitter's guild is a staggering, incredible thing. It is a room filled with men and women who have in common one obsession. They are possessed enough by the manipulation of two pointy needles and some yarn to give up whole free evenings, not just to knit, but to talk about it. The first time you find yourself having a conversation about moss stitch with a group of people who aren't desperately trying to escape you . . . it's like coming home.

*I will join my local club or guild so that I can talk about knitting and still get invited to my friends' parties.*

*Love thy neighbor as yourself,*
*but choose your neighborhood.*
— LOUISE BEAL

When my mother-in-law was a young mother in Newfoundland, Canada, she used to make time each afternoon during the brief summer to sit and knit in the sun. Being a mother, she used to get called into the house often to solve troubles, stir pots, and answer the phone. Often, when she would return to her knitting she would find enormous mistakes: yarn overs, dropped stitches, cables turned round the wrong way. She would ponder these things, chalk them up to losing her mind, and carry on. It was more than 20 years later that her next-door neighbor, Dick, finally admitted that he used to hop the fence and have a go at her knitting.

*Some people have an inner knitter . . .*
*screaming to be heard.*

*I love being married.*
*It's so great to find that one special person*
*you want to annoy for the rest of your life.*
— RITA RUDNER

It took me years and years of trial efforts to work out that there is absolutely no knitting triumph I can achieve that my husband will think is worth being woken up for.

*As strange as I find this, I will try to respect it.*

You know you
knit too much when . . .

You find yourself pondering
the decision about what
knitting to take to the
grocery store with you,
because you might have
to wait in the checkout.

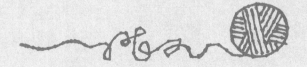

*My masculinity isn't hinged on whether or not I knit.*

— ROBIN GREEN AND MITCHELL BURGESS, *Northern Exposure*

Russell Crowe (actor)
Bob Mackie (designer)
Rosie Greer (football player)
Laurence Fishburne (actor)
Isaac Mizrahi (designer)

Until the beginning of the machine age, knitting guilds were populated only by men. It was when knitting machines were invented that the men went to the factories, and hand knitting fell to women.

*Everything has its beauty
but not everyone sees it.*
— CONFUCIUS

Mohair is unique among fibers in that it possesses a beautiful halo of fuzziness that effectively welds the knitting together. Few and far between are the knitters who can pull back knitting mistakes in mohair with their sanity and sobriety intact. Those who choose to knit with mohair would do well to triple-check that they have cast on the correct number of stitches, because errors are best abandoned. Also note that this yarn quality increases the chances of not noticing a mistake for 8 inches. This chance is upgraded to a virtual certainty if you have only the exact amount of mohair required for the project, or if you paid a crazy amount of money for it.

*If I ever want to knit something that will never, ever come apart, I will choose mohair.*

*Nature always sides with the hidden flaw.*
— MURPHY'S NINTH LAW

Felting — or, more properly, "fulling" — is the act of taking a knitted object and submersing it into hot water and agitating it. The fibers in the wool hook together to form a firm, dense fabric that no longer resembles knitting. This process makes good bags, slippers, and hats. It is only known by its other name, "shrinking," when it is done by accident.

*I will respect the laws of Murphy when allowing my knitting near water.*

*I base most of my fashion taste on
what doesn't itch.*

— GILDA RADNER

There is a certain segment of knitters who refuse to accept that there may be such a thing as a wool allergy. They accept that you can be allergic to bees, peanut butter, daisies, or penicillin, but not their precious wool. They maintain that the allergic have simply not yet met the "right" wool.

*I will try to accept a wool allergy instead of attempting to sneak wool into the wardrobes of the unwilling using unethical subterfuge, just so that I can prove a point.*

*"Anna Makarovna has finished her stocking,"
said Countess Marya. . . . They meant two
stockings, which, by a secret known only
to her, Anna Makarovna used to knit on her
needles simultaneously. When the pair was
finished, she always made a solemn ceremony
of pulling one stocking out of the other
in the presence of the children.*
— LEO TOLSTOY, *War and Peace*

This is accomplished by a technique
known as "double knitting." The
stitches for each of the two socks alter-
nate on the needles, and the knitting is
accomplished by knitting these stitches
with two balls of yarn, alternating balls
with each stitch.

*I wonder whether Anna Makarovna ever
had the experience of discovering that after
hours of painstaking alternation, as she
triumphantly pulled the socks apart, that
they were fused in one spot, joined by one
stinking stitch.*

*Sometimes I can't figure designers out.*
*It's as if they flunked human anatomy.*
— ERMA BOMBECK

Dear designer of questionable intent,

Please send me a photo of yourself. Please be wearing the knitted pants that you designed. It's not that I don't believe that there is anyone out there thin enough to wear horizontally striped trousers knit from chunky wool, it's just that I would like to know whether you are deliberately cruel or whether you are the one woman these would really look great on.

*When choosing projects, I will remember that there are very few derrieres that can stand up to that kind of assault.*

*Only Allah is perfect.*

— PERSIAN LORE

I got to thinking about the Persian rugs woven by masters and how they insert one mistake, to show humility in the face of Allah's perfection. I have often thought that I, too, having knit the perfect sweater, would intentionally insert one little mistake . . . to keep myself humble. I realize now, of course, that I'm out of my mind. I've always made countless mistakes long before the end.

*I will remember this quote and embrace my human imperfection.*

*True beauty dwells in deep retreats,*
*Whose veil is unremoved.*
— WILLIAM WORDSWORTH

There is a simple act that unites all knitters. If you give them a hand-knit sweater, they will turn it inside-out to look at the sewing up of seams and the weaving in of ends. They will do this without even considering how odd it appears to examine closely the wrong side of a garment. This is done partly as a competitive move, an attempt to catch the other knitter with sloppy ends, and partly because knitters know that it is an art. It is not enough to have a sweater that looks good only on the outside. To be truly worthy, the sweater must possess inner beauty.

*I will not wimp out during the sewing up of my knitting. The making up deserves as much attention as the knitting. Someone will be checking.*

*I have not failed. I've just found*
*10,000 ways that won't work.*
— Thomas A. Edison

The first time you turn a heel correctly is a landmark knitting moment. Learning to do the magic trick of turning a corner in three dimensions with your wool and your wits . . . well, you feel pretty clever. Clever enough that the 300 times you ended up with a sock heel you could sell at an old-time circus freak show are magically erased from your memory.

*I will appreciate the clever architecture of a knitted heel.*

*Before I met my husband, I'd never fallen in love, though I'd stepped in it a few times.*
— RITA RUDNER

In Devon, England, during the nineteenth century it was common practice for a bride-to-be to knit a wedding sweater for her beloved. It would be elaborate, of fine wool, and as personal as possible, sometimes even with his initials knit into the gusset under the arms, like an inscription in a ring. The incredible thing was that this sweater was not just a gift but also formal attire that the groom would wear to the wedding.

*There is no occasion too fancy to express your love in wool.*

*The artist is nothing without the gift,*
*but the gift is nothing without work.*
— EMILE ZOLA

Really, there are only two kinds of people who are going to understand about hand-knit socks: those who wear them and know the singular joy of perfect socks, and the knitters who have the pleasure of giving that exquisite experience. Everybody else thinks you must be a special kind of crazy to spend so much time making something that you could buy for $1.99 at the store.

*The only way to educate the masses is to knit for them.*

*If evolution really works, how come mothers only have two hands?*
— MILTON BERLE

Many women discover their urge to knit when expecting a baby. It seems like the right thing to do, knitting little baby things to wrap your new arrival in. When you think about it, being a new knitter and being a new mother are a lot alike. Both activities get better with practice, both are awkward and bumpy at the beginning, and both yield lovely results using common materials.

*Done right, motherhood and knitting are both creative acts.*

# Advice for a new knitter:

When choosing a pattern, look for ones that have words such as "simple," "basic," and "easy."

If you see the words "intriguing," "challenging," or "intricate," look elsewhere.

If you happen across a pattern that says "heirloom," slowly put down the pattern and back away.

*"Heirloom" is knitting code for "This pattern is so difficult that you would consider death a relief."*

*There is a very fine line between
"hobby" and "mental illness."*
— DAVE BARRY

It's difficult for those who live with passionate knitters. From time to time, they might even consider us odd. Every time my husband starts talking about how crazy I am to like knitting this much, I remind him . . . it could be worse. What if I were this interested in cabbage?

*I will not let the non-knitters of the world decide how normal I am.*

*All children are essentially criminal.*
— DENIS DIDEROT

Attention: children of knitters. Here are five possible strategies to torment your knitting parent.

1. Refuse to wear anything knitted at all. Ever, no matter how sophisticated the bribe.
2. Repeatedly use knitting needles for purposes that render them useless for knitting — like, say . . . digging in the sandbox.
3. Grow, preferably faster than your designated knitter can knit.
4. Deeply desire a sweater in only a neon rainbow variegated yarn that is so bright that it causes nausea and dizziness to the knitter.
5. Intentionally develop a wool allergy.

*Sweater, n.: garment worn by child
when its mother is feeling chilly.*

— AMBROSE BIERCE

I was in the park and there was a baby in a carriage under a tree. I walked by and I could tell in an instant. This baby was the child of a knitter. This baby was wrapped in love that was measured by the stitch. Bonnet, sweater, blanket, bootees, and leggings of smooth wool. If it wasn't for the obvious love that this baby was wrapped in, I would have felt sorry for it. It was 80°F out.

*I will not allow something as changeable as the seasons to keep me from expressing my love in wool.*

*It is not fair to ask of others what you are not willing to do yourself.*

— ELEANOR ROOSEVELT

I'm reasonably sure that Calvin Klein does not knit. I recently got a pattern for knitting an impossibly beautiful sweater that Calvin designed, and after several crazy-making hours I've decided there is no way that Calvin himself has ever sat down with a pair of needles, because there's no way he would do this to me if he had. I could be wrong, and if I am could somebody get Calvin to call me? I'm stuck on row 7.

*I will not trust the non-knitting to write my patterns. They know nothing of knitterly suffering.*

*Creative minds have always been known to
survive any kind of bad training.*

— ANNA FREUD

There is no wrong way to knit.
The debate between throwing the
yarn and picking it, using circulars
or straights, choosing Fair Isle or
intarsia . . . it's all a moot point. If you
get something knitted at the end of it,
you are doing it right. We should all
agree to stop correcting each other and
deal with the more important issue.
How wrong crochet is.

*I will resist the temptation to correct another
knitter.*

*The important thing is
not to stop questioning.*

— ALBERT EINSTEIN

**3** questions for a knitter having trouble:

1. Have you checked the pattern for errors?
2. Is there any possibility that you are misunderstanding the pattern?
3. Are you sure that you wouldn't be happier if you buried it under a large oak tree in the park?

*Forgive your enemies,*
*but never forget their names.*
— John Fitzgerald Kennedy

*Tinea pellionella:*
the casemaking clothes moth

*Tineola bisselliella:*
the common clothes moth

*Anthrenus verbasci:*
the common carpet beetle

*I will remain ever vigilant to the*
*enemies of wool.*

*Until he extends the circle of*
*his compassion to all living things,*
*man will not himself find peace.*
— ALBERT SCHWEITZER

As I go through my daily life, I try hard to have respect for every life I encounter. I attempt not to devalue a life because it is small or seemingly trivial; I remember that each living thing, from an ant to a whale, fills a vital role in the circle of life. The balance and health of the planet hinges on a delicate and largely mysterious web of life, where the fate of a single ant could affect us all.

I try to remember this especially when I see a moth in my stash and am overcome with the overwhelming urge to squash the living daylights out of it and every single member of its family.

*I will try to remember that moths are to wool as yin is to yang and try to respect them as a species with a right to be here.*

*We live in a moment of history*
*where change is so speeded up*
*that we begin to see the present*
*only when it is already disappearing.*
— R. D. LAING

We live in world of machines. Our world moves faster, bigger, and better with every moment. Machines replace humans and often do our jobs better.

When you are knitting socks and sweaters and scarves, you aren't just knitting. You are assigning a value to human effort. You are holding back time. You are preserving the simple unchanging act of handwork.

*I will remember that knitting is more mean-ingful than it seems.*

*A rolling stone gathers no moss.*
— PROVERB

The fourteenth law of yarn dictates that a rolling ball of yarn will only gather moss if it is not green wool. White wool will gather anything black or red, such as dog hair or red wine, whereas black wool will gather chalk dust. Should the knitter be color-blind, the yarn will gather gum. A rolling ball of yarn will also roll as far away from you as possible, likely out of the car, down the aisle of the church (where you hoped no one would notice you were knitting), or into any available liquid.

*I will stay alert to all yarn strategies. I will choose beverages that match my project.*

*Properly practiced, knitting soothes
the troubled spirit, and it doesn't hurt
the untroubled spirit, either.*
— Elizabeth Zimmerman

In the nineteenth century, knitting was prescribed to women as a cure for nervousness and hysteria. Many new knitters find this sort of hard to believe because, until you get good at it, knitting seems to cause those ailments.

*The twitch above my right eye will disappear with knitting practice.*

*To be without some of the things you want is*
*an indispensable part of happiness.*
— BERTRAND RUSSELL

I hear all kinds of things about specific yarns that make me want them. Yarn A is so soft, Yarn B comes in an incredible heathered blue, Yarn C is light as a feather. I can be tempted by the things I see other knitters make from a certain yarn, coerced by an incredible colorway or texture of a yarn. Nothing, however, will impel me to spend hours and hours of time and tons of money faster than hearing that a yarn is "discontinued."

*There will be another yarn like this one someday. I do not need to buy all I can find of this one.*

*All's fair in love and war.*
— FRANCIS EDWARD SMEDLEY

Overheard at a yarn shop sale:

Knitter A: "This is a beautiful yarn.
I wonder how it knits up."
Knitter B: "That? I heard it's horrible.
Splits while you knit it and pills
when you wash it. Sort of a funny
color isn't it?"
Knitter A: "Really? Well, it's probably not
worth the trouble, even at 50 percent
off." (*Wanders off.*)

Knitter B was seen shortly thereafter
at the cash desk with ALL of the yarn in
question, scoring it at 50 percent off.

*Do you want the yarn or not?*

*Sleep that knits up the*
*ravelled sleave of care*
*The death of each day's life,*
*sore labour's bath*
*Balm of hurt minds,*
*great nature's second course,*
*Chief nourisher in life's feast.*
— WILLIAM SHAKESPEARE, *Macbeth*

I don't know of even one knitter who does not hope, either actively or secretly, to learn to knit in her sleep.

*Should I fall asleep with my knitting in my hands, I will remember to check for signs of progress when I wake up.*

*Lead us not into temptation.*
*Just tell us where it is; we'll find it.*
— SAM LEVENSON

I cannot count the number of times I have been in a yarn shop. Hundreds, probably thousands of times. I can count on one hand the number of times I left with nothing: three. Once because I'd forgotten my money, once because my child felt ill, and once because my credit card was declined. (It was the second yarn shop of the day.)

*Even the worst yarn shop has something you need.*

*We cannot waste time.*
*We can only waste ourselves.*
— GEORGE M. ADAMS

Sometimes, people come up to me when I am knitting and they say things like, "Oh, I wish I could knit, but I'm just not the kind of person who can sit and waste time like that." How can knitting be wasting time? First, I never just knit; I knit and think, knit and listen, knit and watch. Second, you aren't wasting time if you get a useful or beautiful object at the end of it.

*I will remember that not everyone under-stands. I will resist the urge to ask others what they do when they watch TV.*

*Comedy is tragedy plus time.*
— CAROL BURNETT

I remember this one gray sweater. I used the last of a discontinued yarn and spent hours pouring over magazines and books to find the pattern that would do it justice. I spent hours knitting it, and it dragged out into a project that took months. I was meticulous; I corrected every mistake, pulled back every sloppy stitch. When it was finally finished, I spent more time scouring the city for the exact, perfect buttons; the ones that would allow the wonder and the glory of this sweater to shine for all time.

When it was done, I put it on the bed so that I could admire it as I passed by. Immediately thereafter, my husband, doing one of the four loads of laundry he has done in our marriage, shrunk it into oblivion.

*Sometimes, time does not heal all wounds, but it can get you out of doing the laundry.*

*Join, being careful not to twist.*
— KNITTING PATTERNS

The chances of being able to join a multitude of stitches on a circular needle without twisting them and knitting a freak of geometry are influenced by the following variables:

- The number of stitches
- The amount of time allotted to perform the task
- The material being knitted

*Taking these rules into account, I understand that the odds of joining 300 stitches in my sister's mohair birthday sweater without twisting them are just about zero.*

*USA Today has come out with a new survey:*
*Apparently three out of four people make up*
*75 percent of the population.*
— DAVID LETTERMAN

I was surprised recently to discover that the majority of sock knitters darn socks the way I do. Considering how many hours of hard work are in a pair of socks, there are not many knitters who would merely throw a pair away because they have a hole in them. Most use my darning technique, which consists of loudly exclaiming DARN and a few other choice expletives before dropping them in the garbage.

*I will forgive myself for preferring knitting to darning.*

*A #6 aluminum needle has been known to furnish an excellent emergency shearpin for an outboard motor.*

— ELIZABETH ZIMMERMAN

Other uses for knitting needles:

- Cake tester (when knitting needle comes out clean, the cake is done)
- Stir stick
- Back scratcher
- Lock pick for the bathroom door when your three-year-old is in there alone and you can hear repeated flushing and a very angry cat

*Really, if you carry these things around all the time, you find a lot of uses for them.*

*Isn't it awful that cold feet make for a cold imagination and that a pair of woollen socks induce good thoughts!*
— FRANZ GRILLPARZER

4 reasons to knit socks:

1. Hand-knit socks are the most comfortable socks anyone will ever wear.
2. Knitting socks has passed virtually unchanged through history. You are doing what knitters have done for hundreds of years.
3. Turning a heel makes you feel smart.
4. Sock projects are portable and fit in a pocket or bag.

*Finally, an impressive finished project that is beautiful, functional, comfortable, and a historic lesson can be had for the cost of only two balls of yarn.*

You know you
knit too much when . . .

You cite the fact that
knitting burns about
90 calories an hour, not
allowing extra for style,
conviction, and retrieving
your ball of yarn from
under the couch.

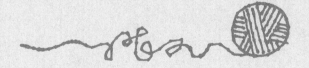

*Most people want to be delivered from temptation but would like it to keep in touch.*

— ROBERT ORBEN

I sign up for every yarn catalog I can. I get them in the mail, I pore over them, I drink my coffee, and I imagine ordering lovely things from all the wonderful places. The interesting thing is that I continue to get the catalogs, even to renew my place on the mailing list . . . from shops that carry nothing I would ever use. I even get catalogs from shops that I openly mock, and if these shops stop mailing me the thing (presumably because I have never bought anything), I will phone and insist that they begin mailing it again.

*Never look away from a yarn opportunity.*

*Some are kissing mothers*
*and some are scolding mothers,*
*but it is love just the same.*
— PEARL S. BUCK

On very cold days, when I pull my daughter's hand-knit sweater over her head or when I watch her play in the snow with warm mittens on, I feel like a good mother. There is just something about knowing that my children are warm because I knitted them something that feeds my motherly soul.

*I hope that it makes up for all the times I said I'd help them after "one more row."*

*If you're crazy, there's two things you*
*can do to make yourself feel better:*
*one is to get yourself cured.*
*The other is to make everyone you*
*have to deal with crazy.*
— ALAN DEAN FOSTER

Have you ever wondered whether some designs are really just complicated jokes? I mean, maybe the designers didn't really plan for anyone to ever knit them. Perhaps they are sitting by a pool, far away, chuckling to themselves at the very thought of you suffering a breakdown trying to knit their patterns.

*I will resist the urge to try and look up their phone numbers to ask them.*

*My second favorite household chore is ironing.*
*My first being hitting my head on the top*
*bunk bed until I faint.*
— ERMA BOMBECK

My knitting is in a constant state of competition with the household chores. After years and years of painful juggling, I have almost completely decided to give up on the housework. The way I see it, I can always clean up the house when I am old, but I'll never get this knitting time back.

*Remember, dusting requires the same arm movement whether it has been a week or a month.*

*Black holes are where God divided by zero.*
— STEVEN WRIGHT

Every knitter knows about the knitterly version of a black hole. This is an error in the time-space continuum centered around the process of knitting your sweater. Every knitter knows when he has found it. You measure your knitting and discover that it is 12 inches long. You knit for an hour, remeasure, and discover that your knitting is still 12 inches long. You knit what must surely be 200 rows, measure again, and discover that your knitting is 12 inches long. Science has yet to prove that a woolly black hole exists, but it's only a matter of time.

*You are not crazy; you are experiencing a scientific mystery.*

*It's easy to stop making mistakes.*
*Just stop having ideas.*

— Anonymous

The first thing you should think when you notice that you used the wrong yarn color 12 rows back on your complex Fair Isle sweater is that there is no shame in knitting an "interpretation" of a pattern.

*I am so creative that innovative design happens by accident.*

*Measure twice, cut once.*

— CARPENTER'S RULE

Many Fair Isle sweaters incorporate "steeks." This technique allows the knitter to knit the body of the sweater completely in the round, without dividing the work into a front and back and having to work back and forth. The knitter works straight up to the shoulders, returning later to cut openings for the sleeves. The instructions sometimes ask the knitter to sew a row (or two) of stitching around this opening, but if the sweater is worked with wool that clings well to itself, the steek is simply cut open with no preparation.

*No matter which method you use it is normal to feel varying levels of nausea, hysteria, and dizziness during the process of cutting into a sweater.*

*Control thy passions, lest they
take vengeance on thee.*
— Epictetus

In case you were wondering, if you are
making a Norwegian sweater and you
measure the sleeve to determine your
armhole depth, and then very, very carefully mark that depth onto your sweater
body, then take out the sewing machine
and carefully sew two lines of stitching
around your steeks, then discover that
you made them the wrong length
because you measured only one of the
sleeves and that sleeve is inexplicably
4 inches wider than its mate . . . it takes
17 hours to unpick that machine
stitching.

*I will try to recognize that cursing for the
entire 17 hours will do little to help.*

*That it will never come again*
*Is what makes life so sweet.*
— EMILY DICKINSON

Occasionally, while knitting something particularly yummy I feel about my knitting as I do about a good book. I look and see that there are only a few pages left and feel sorry that there won't be more of it. The same goes for a brilliant yarn. In fact, I'm often reluctant to knit up my favorites, because when I am done knitting them, I won't have the yarn anymore. Sure, I'll have a sweater, but it's not the same. The yarn will be gone forever.

*I will resist the urge to hoard my favorite yarns forever, constantly trying to determine whether the projects they are intended for are "worthy."*

*I wasted time, and now doth time waste me.*
— WILLIAM SHAKESPEARE

I am sitting alone in the darkened living room. It is 4:00 A.M. on Christmas morning, and my family will be up in a few hours to see what Santa has brought. I am frantically knitting. It is the same every year; over and over I am brought to my knees by this enormous knitting deadline and end up weeping into my eggnog, trying to finish knitting presents by daybreak. There must be something wrong with me. Christmas isn't a surprise; it's on the same day every year. Every year I tell myself, this year will be different.

Then every year, it's me and Santa, down to the wire.

*I will try to recognize that some people on my list would prefer that I were coherent, healthy, and sane on Christmas morning, rather than delirious but finished with the damn hat.*

*If the minimum wasn't acceptable it
wouldn't be called the minimum.*
— GEORGE MUNCASTER

My husband, in an incredible show of love, is knitting me a sock. He has been working on it (on and off) for about five years, painstakingly knitting round after round. He curses, rubs his eyes, drops needles, and complains bitterly about the impending heel (he probably has another two years before he has to worry about that), but he is knitting. He has always referred to this process as knitting me "a sock," and the perceptive among you will note that "sock" is singular. He has never promised a pair.

*Should my husband ever finish my "sock," I will wear it proudly (and singularly) for all of my days. He is my mate; my sock doesn't need one.*

*When you see a married couple*
*walking down the street, the one that's*
*a few steps ahead is the one that's mad.*
— HELEN ROWLAND

My husband, lovely and patient man that he is, has sustained several injuries related to my knitting. He has a small scar on his foot, the result of a puncture wound incurred when I left my sock knitting on the floor. He cringes when he thinks of the darning needle accidentally left on the couch seat when I was making his sweater, and he flinches visibly when he thinks about the various times he has been accidentally stabbed with sundry and assorted knitting needles or been tripped by careless yarn placement. My friends think he tolerates this out of love. My knitting friends know better.

*He is doing it for the sweaters.*

*I'm not obsessed, I'm just highly preoccupied.*
— ANONYMOUS

Self-patterning sock yarn is very, very neat. It is dyed to produce stripes or a pattern meant to resemble Fair Isle when you knit it up. It can be fun and interesting to work with, but be warned. For those inclined to be obsessive, it can lead to a dangerous fixation with making sure the two socks match. Many a fine knitter has gone down the twitchy path of trying to compensate for dyeing errors or normal variations in the yarn in order to come up with two socks that are precisely the same. I have no proof, but I suspect that this may be a yarn manufacturer's idea of a joke.

*I will accept that some sock yarns simply produce fraternal rather than identical twins.*

# Swift:

*a twirling reel used to hold a skein
of yarn as it is wound into a ball.*

A swift is a tool used to replace your
friends and family. Clever knitters
will procure one the first time their
mates or children refuse to hold the
skein of yarn for them, thus reducing
the number of yarn-related disputes
in the family environment. Swifts also
reduce knitter injury by eliminating
awkward and dangerous attempts to
hold your own skein of yarn with your
feet while winding with your hands.
There are anecdotal reports that swifts
may reduce tangling and cursing related
to using household furniture for swift-
like purposes.

*To save time, sanity, and my marriage, I will
consider purchasing the right tools for the job.*

*Think for yourself and let others
enjoy the privilege of doing so too.*
— VOLTAIRE

My friend Sharon proudly pulled out her first project: a red sweater. She was halfway up the back, and she held out the knitting to me, smiling. Sharon explained that the sweater was done in stockinette stitch, but it looked funny to me. On closer examination I discovered that Sharon had twisted each and every stitch. The stitch was pretty, but it wasn't stockinette. I praised the sweater, then showed Sharon the mistake she was making and pulled out my knitting to teach her how to make a proper stitch. Sharon was uninterested. "Don't you want to be a better knitter?" I queried.

"I just want to knit," she replied. "I don't have to be good."

*I will respect that not everybody needs to be perfect. Sometimes, just knitting is enough.*

*I have a hat. It is graceful and feminine and gives me a certain dignity, as if I were attending a state funeral or something. Someday I may get up enough courage to wear it, instead of carrying it.*

— ERMA BOMBECK

# 5 reasons to knit hats:

1. They are a small project. You can go nuts with a fiber you usually couldn't afford, such as cashmere or alpaca.
2. A great deal of body heat is lost through the head.
3. A great hat can make up for bad hair.
4. They can be knit fairly quickly and, as a bonus, children's heads grow slowly compared to the rest of them.
5. Normally timid dressers (even male ones) will often wear a wild hat. Your inner artist can be fully released through hat knitting without the fear that it will never be worn.

> *Whoever said money can't buy happiness*
> *simply didn't know where to go shopping.*
> — BO DEREK

There is a segment of my stash that I cannot explain. If you knew me, and you looked at this yarn, you would think that I had gone to the yarn store drunk. There is pink chenille (I wouldn't be caught dead in this pink, and I hate chenille), there is heavy cotton (cotton is my enemy; knitting it makes my hands hurt), and so on. I offer this only by way of explanation. It turns out that I will buy any yarn, even yarn I will never use, if the store discounts it by more than 50 percent.

*Do not be tricked. Not all yarn is meant to be yours, no matter how good a deal it is.*

*The great aim of education
is not knowledge but action.*
— HERBERT SPENCER

My mother is an avid garage sale shopper. She enjoys finding little treasures and getting good deals. She loves a $2 lamp the way that I love knitting. She called me one weekend after making her neighborhood rounds and described some yarn she had seen at a sale. "It was a lovely green," she said, "and the label said 100 percent Shetland wool . . . there were 12 skeins for $4." The world swirled around me excitedly. "Did you get it?" I asked, suddenly understanding completely what my mother sees in garage sales. "No," she replied, "I wasn't sure if it was good wool."

*Educate your family and friends. Teach them this: there is no such thing as "bad" $4 wool.*

You know you
knit too much when . . .

You find yourself stalking
a man in the grocery store,
not because he's really
good-looking, but because
he is wearing an Aran
sweater with a cable you
are trying to work out.

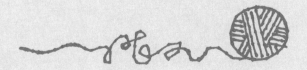

*I have long been of the opinion that if work were such a splendid thing the rich would have kept more of it for themselves.*

— BRUCE GROCOTT

Knitting has many rewards. Sometimes it is the joy of wondrous creativity, of taking yarn and needles and making a new and beautiful thing out of nothing. Sometimes it is figuring out something tricky and clever, solving a problem with your wits and your wool. There is even the joy of clothing your loved ones or wrapping a baby in a blanket you made yourself. Sometimes, though, it is the pride of having slogged through 26 inches of plain boring garter stitch, row after mind-numbingly plain row, and coming out the other side with your sanity and desire to remain a knitter intact.

*I will pride myself on my stamina as a knitter.*

*He who would travel happily*
*must travel light.*
— Antoine de Saint-Exupery

It used to be that when I traveled, I packed lightly enough that I would have room left in my suitcase to bring back souvenir yarn purchases. Then I met a brilliant woman who was shopping wholeheartedly at a sheep and wool festival, and I kidded her about needing to buy another suitcase to get it all home. "No way," she said. "Tomorrow before I get on the plane I'm going to mail it all to myself."

*Respect your fellow travelers. They have much to teach you.*

*They're here for a long, long time.*
*They'll have to make the best of things,*
*it's an uphill climb.*

— SHERWOOD SCHWARTZ
AND GEORGE WYLE,
"Ballad of Gilligan's Island"

Imagine this: You are shipwrecked on an island with only the knitting that you had with you on the boat.

When you are done knitting it, and have nothing more to knit, do you unravel the work and start again, just to have something to knit? If so, you are a process knitter. You knit for the pleasure of knitting.

If you imagine that, upon finishing, you put on the sweater and go look for wild grasses that you could knit into a tent or a hammock, you are a product knitter. You knit for the pleasure of the finished item.

*I will respect my type and pack for boat trips accordingly, because you never know.*

*Just say no to drugs.*
— Nancy Reagan

North America spends billions of dollars each year giving us the message that some drugs are a slippery slope. One taste of a seemingly harmless substance can lead to wrack and ruin for some people. Yet, no one ever tells a knitter that one taste of the luxury fiber qiviut can lead to an unreasonable desire to stalk the wild musk ox under the Arctic moon, trying to get just a little bit more.

*I will be careful to limit my exposure to exotic and fabulous fibers. It's a slippery slope.*

*Your best teacher is your last mistake.*
— RALPH NADER

I cannot count the number of times that after using the "long-tail" method to cast on, I have picked up the tail and begun knitting with it instead of the working yarn. Luckily, this is a mistake that you realize pretty quickly. Once, however, after finishing one ball of yarn and intending to begin another, I very, very carefully spliced the working yarn to the long tail. You don't forget that as quickly.

*I will remember, while I am undoing my mistake, that the ability to make a really sturdy splice is a double-edged sword.*

*People seem to enjoy things more*
*when they know a lot of other people*
*have been left out of the pleasure.*
— RUSSELL BAKER

At my favorite yarn shop there was the best yarn ever. It was soft, it was cheap, and it moved through a range of colors in each skein, providing me with endless entertainment. I made a shawl from it, and the shawl became one of my favorites. I was very proud of it, but I showed it to no other knitters. The yarn had been discontinued and I couldn't afford to buy it all, but I knew that if my knitting friends discovered it, they would buy it and there would be less left for me. I purchased the remaining stock over the course of a few months, then showed off my shawl. I'm not proud of what I did, but the important thing is that I got all the yarn.

*I will strive to be a more generous person,*
*but I might not start with this yarn.*

*I have noticed that the people who are late are often so much jollier than the people who have to wait for them.*

— E.V. Lucas

If the world were run by knitters, then it would be laid out with bars and libraries next to yarn shops so that your mate would be happy to pop next door and wait for you.

*Until knitters run the world, I will accept that asking my mate to drive me to the yarn shop might not be to my advantage.*

You know you
knit too much when . . .

You discover that the
airline you booked your
flight with does not allow
knitting needles on board
and you seriously consider
changing carriers, because
you don't know whether
you can sit for seven hours
without knitting.

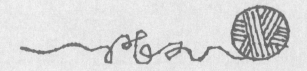

*Let us watch well our beginnings,*
*and results will manage themselves.*
— ALEXANDER CLARK

There are several methods for ensuring that you cast on the right number of stitches. Some knitters use stitch markers placed every 10 stitches; others make notes on a piece of paper at regular intervals. I cast on the approximate number, then count them as many times as it takes to get the right number twice.

*Sometimes this is a long process. I will remember that if I choose to make things difficult for myself I can't complain.*

*The man who goes farthest is generally
the one who is willing to do and dare.
The sure-thing boat never gets far from shore.*
— DALE CARNEGIE

The "sure thing" in knitting is a myth.
There is no way, none — even if you
have knit a thousand things, a million
yards, or a billion socks — that your
knitting will not find a way to punish
you if you dare to get cocky.

Saying out loud things such as "I know
this yarn so well, I don't need to do a
swatch" or "I never use a pattern" invites
disaster. Even if your gauge is perfect or
you remember the pattern with total
recall, cockiness will not be tolerated by
the celestial powers that rule knitting.

*If I am foolish enough to be arrogant about
my knitting, I will understand when it spon-
taneously bursts into flames.*

*Truly, to tell lies is not honorable;*
*But when the truth entails tremendous ruin,*
*To speak dishonorably is pardonable.*
— SOPHOCLES

There is always something redeeming about a knitted piece. Perhaps it is not the color, or pattern, or form . . . but there must be something. Nothing knitted can be truly horrible. When I am asked my opinion of a piece of knitting that I truly regard as ugly, I do not lie; I find the truths that I can tell without hurting the feelings of the knitter. My favorite is, "Wow, that looks like a lot of work!" Or, "My goodness, that's such a personal work of art."

*There is no such thing as worthless knitting, simply knitting that is really not to your taste.*

*Do not worry about your difficulties
in mathematics. I can assure you
mine are still greater.*
— ALBERT EINSTEIN

I failed 10th grade math four times. I hate mathematics so much that the very thought of a return to it in any form is enough to make me want to run away to Belize, screaming all the way. It is a deeply bitter truth that knitting has math in it. Division to place increases, addition to enlarge, subtraction to shrink, even some multiplication to work out how many times a Fair Isle motif will fit across a row. If you want to be a knitter, there is going to be some math. It is incredible to me that the very same computations that made me want to claw my eyes out in math class are completely worthwhile in knitting.

*Why couldn't they have used knitting to teach me math in 10th grade?*

*Marriage is a wonderful institution,*
*but who would want to live*
*in an institution?*
— H. L. MENCKEN

The best reason for a knitter to marry is that you can't teach the cat to be impressed when you finish a lace scarf.

*Even if he doesn't know a cable from a bobble, my mate can be my biggest cheerleader.*

*Stress is an ignorant state. It believes
that everything is an emergency.
Nothing is that important.*
— NATALIE GOLDBERG

**3** ways to tell that knitting deadlines are getting to you:

❶ You are knitting the gift for the birthday girl on the way to the party.

❷ You have decided that replacing sleep with knitting just makes sense.

❸ You have calculated the number of stitches remaining in the project and think that it's "pretty normal" that you are counting down.

*What difference does it make how much
you have? What you do not have
amounts to much more.*

— SENECA

The world is full of knitters who are driven to collect yarn by an inner voice that tells them there will never be enough. They have more yarn than they could ever use in a lifetime, even if they quit their jobs and knit full-time until they died. The world is full of non-knitters who think this is odd.

*I will remember, when challenged by a non-knitter who has concerns about my yarn stash, that no one ever said, "Hey, Michelangelo, don't you think you're getting carried away with this paint thing?"*

*Marriage has no guarantees.*
*If that's what you're looking for,*
*go live with a car battery.*
— ERMA BOMBECK

For years my husband showed no interest in my knitting. In fact, the overwhelming presence of yarn seemed to bug him. Then I began knitting him dress socks.

*If your mate doesn't understand your knitting habit, then maybe he hasn't been properly bribed yet.*

*We cannot command Nature*
*except by obeying her.*
— FRANCIS BACON

So the rumors were true; there it was, sitting innocently on the shelf. Yarn made from corn. Called "Ingeo," the yarn is made from the starches and sugars of corn and converted to a natural resin that is spun into yarn. The resulting fiber is biodegradable and can be composted to return the nutrients to the soil. It is soft, lovely, and a completely renewable resource.

*Although I embrace fiber technologies that protect the Earth, I will remember that wearing an Ingeo tank top to a goat farm might have disastrous results.*

*One of the greatest discoveries a man makes,*
*one of his great surprises, is to find he can*
*do what he was afraid he couldn't do.*
— HENRY FORD

I was surprised to discover that there
are timid knitters — knitters who are
afraid to do lace, afraid to do cables,
afraid of making a mistake or taking
on a big project. I was shocked. Afraid?
Be afraid of skydiving. Be afraid of wild
boar. Be fearless with knitting.

*I will remember that no one has ever been*
*killed or maimed by being adventurous with*
*knitting, no matter how pointy the needles.*

*Progress might have been all right once,*
*but it has gone on too long.*
— OGDEN NASH

If you hunt around, you will find yarns made of some pretty strange stuff. The one that boggles my mind most is the superfine yarn made from stainless steel. Combined with other fibers, such as wool, cotton, and linen, it's more approachable than you would think.

*As much as I will try to accept progress and things such as stainless-steel yarn, I still find it remarkable that after I knit a sweater I could whip into the kitchen and shine my pots with it.*

You know you
knit too much when . . .

You put your computer
keyboard on the floor while
reading your daily e-mails
so you can hit the spacebar
with your toe to scroll
through them while knitting.

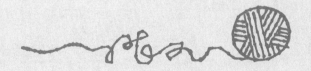

*To win without risk is to triumph*
*without glory.*
— PIERRE CORNEILLE

Faced with a major knitting mistake, such as a miscrossed cable, I have three basic choices. I could ignore it; pull the work back and re-knit it; or go wild, drop the offending stitches, and painstakingly spend hours with a crochet hook tediously fixing just those few. Knitting is not necessarily the most daring of hobbies, certainly not compared to eating fire or something like that, but those of us who need thrills in our lives and have a bit of a competitive edge embrace these chances to really go out on a limb.

*It's not necessarily the smart thing to do, but there's really nothing like conceiving and executing an insane feat of repair and having it work.*

*People want economy and they will pay
any price to get it.*

— LEE IACOCCA

When I took up spinning, my husband worried that it was just going to devolve into another addiction. To make him feel a little better I pointed out how much money I was going to save spinning my own yarn. Then I bought a spinning wheel, carders, fleece, and dye.

*I will remember that timing is everything, and I might have wanted to make my point sometime after I had spent all that money getting set up and spinning a $500 skein of lumpy yarn.*

*Modesty is a vastly overrated virtue.*
— John Kenneth Galbraith

The knitting magazine had a very beautiful sweater, creatively worked with an openwork mesh stitch. I wanted it badly and planned to make it, until I had a rare flash of insight and realized that a woman who manages to find her bra only for "special occasions" might not really be all that suited to a mesh sweater.

*Knitter, know thyself.*

*It sometimes happens, even in the best
of families, that a baby is born.
This is not necessarily cause for alarm.
The important thing is to keep your wits
about you and borrow some money.*
— ELINOR GOULDING SMITH

When knitting for babies, remember that they have surprisingly large heads. For neckholes in sweaters, I suggest that you follow this rule. First, make the neckline twice the size that seems reasonable to you. Then add a slit and buttons . . . then prepare to be disappointed that the baby grew since you last checked the size.

*I will remember that it is the cautious, and quick, knitter who makes stuff for babies.*

*Honest criticism is hard to take,*
*particularly from a relative, a friend,*
*an acquaintance, or a stranger.*
— FRANKLIN P. JONES

There is one knitter in my guild who is a wonder. Her work is always incredible, her stitches even, her sense of color perfection. She gives workshops and people line up to get in, anxious to elevate their knitting to her level. At one workshop she was explaining that we should all strive for absolutely even stitches. Your work, properly done, should look like it was machine knit. The knitter next to me heaved a sigh and quietly muttered, "Honestly, why wouldn't I just get a knitting machine?"

*Knitting is a human activity. It's okay if it looks like a human did it.*

*You cannot truly listen to anyone and do anything else at the same time.*
— M. Scott Peck

People who knit have long been trying to convince people who don't that they can knit and listen at the same time. Studies have shown that people often show increased focus and even demonstrate greater recollection while knitting.

*Conversely, with some people, knitting is the only thing that gets us through listening to them.*

*Habit, if not resisted, soon becomes necessity.*
— St. Augustine

There is a longstanding joke in our family about what it would take to keep me from knitting. I have knit through illness, disaster, injury, and labor.

When I was expecting my first baby, I asked my midwife when I should call her to come. "When you don't want to knit anymore," she replied.

My husband thought that would be cutting it pretty close.

*In retrospect, I think the midwife should have said, "When you can't keep track of the pattern."*

*If a dog jumps in your lap, it is because
he is fond of you; but if a cat does the same
thing, it is because your lap is warmer.*
— ALFRED NORTH

Although there are few pictures prettier than that of a knitter working happily in his favorite chair, devoted cat by his side, knitters know the truth. The chance that your pet will stay by your side and off your knitting is relative to the pet/project relationship. If you are knitting a brown sweater and own a brown cat, your devoted companion will stand by, but never "on," your knitting. If, however, you own a black cat and are knitting a white shawl, your cat and the project will be inseparable.

*I will try to understand that if I don't bother
to coordinate my projects with my pet, my
pet will be driven to do it for me.*

*Give no decision till both sides thou'st heard.*
— PHOCYLIDES

Knitting needles come in different materials. Wood, ebony, metal, plastic . . . there are many different kinds, and I'm told they all have their uses. I love sharp metal ones, and no one can tell me that there is a point (pun intended) to any other kind. I feel that the slipperiness makes me a faster knitter, and unlike the more fragile wooden ones, I've never broken a metal needle by sitting on it. On the downside, that particular mishap with metal needles can require a tetanus shot.

*I will try other knitting needles, particularly if one type consistently sends me to the emergency room.*

*You don't get harmony when everybody*
*sings the same note.*
— DOUG FLOYD

As long as there has been knitting there have been battles about it. There are self-declared "yarn snobs," who frown on using anything but natural fibers; "gauge snobs," who wouldn't be caught dead with chunky yarn; and "experience snobs," who claim you can't declare yourself a real knitter until you abandon novelty yarns. The truth is that the knitting world is a tiny metaphor for the real world. It takes all kinds.

*I will not allow myself to feel bad if someone disapproves of my knitting. I will also resist the urge to stuff his mailbox full of chunky acrylic fun fur at 3:00 a.m.*

5 things to keep in your knitting bag:

1. A crochet hook for picking up dropped stitches
2. A yarn needle
3. A measuring tape
4. A photocopy of your pattern
5. A fair bit of chocolate or hard liquor, depending on the project

*I will recognize that being prepared will make me a better knitter.*

*One of the few pieces of Newfoundland knitting in a museum is a pair of long underwear dated 1900 and collected by Dorothy Burnham for the Canadian Museum of Civilization. They were knit of homespun wool in an outport [a remote fishing village].*

— GLORIA HICKEY

Can you imagine the whole knitted long underwear thing? In many (cold) parts of the world, knitted long johns were commonplace, and necessary. Whole pants and shirts were knitted of wool so fine that the garments didn't bunch up under your clothes. I don't know whom I feel sorriest for: the knitter who had miles of underwear to knit, the poor soul responsible for hand washing it all, or the desperate victim who had to wear the itchy homespun next to his most delicate parts.

You know you
knit too much when . . .

You think that a stitch or
row counter you could work
with your feet is a really
brilliant idea.

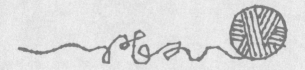

*God gave us our memories so that*
*we might have roses in December.*
— J. M. BARRIE

Some of my stash is silly little balls of yarn that non-knitters (and some knitters) think I'm out of my mind to keep. Here's what they don't know: The white is the yarn I used to knit the baby blanket I wrapped my first baby in. The blue is from the sweater my husband wore on the boat on our anniversary. The purple is from socks my second daughter wore the first day of school. The pink is from the scarf my youngest learned to knit on. They are soft yards of wool, each one a postcard from the life I had while knitting.

*People may laugh at me, but I will remember that some of them collect rocks.*

*It is essential to use X brand yarn*
*to achieve these results.*

— EVERY PATTERN PUT OUT
BY A YARN COMPANY

I was in a crowded and bustling yarn shop when I overheard a young and attractive woman utter this sentence out loud.

"It's too bad that you can't substitute yarns in a pattern; none of these colors really appeals to me."

The silence that descended upon the yarn shop was complete. Heads swivelled around to get a look at her. Knitter after knitter stared incomprehensibly at her. Moments later, as we all recovered, the woman was virtually crushed as we rushed to her side to enlighten her.

*I will remember that substituting yarns is not only possible, but, at times, virtually demanded.*

*Inanimate objects are classified scientifically
into three major categories — those that
don't work, those that break down
and those that get lost.*
— RUSSELL BAKER

Every knitter knows that yarn needles disappear at a rate competitive with socks. I've bought hundreds, lost them all over my house, and have never, ever found one. They are simply gone.

I know that I can't be alone with this problem because often, when I go to buy more from the yarn shop, they are sold out.

I imagine that in five hundred years, when the archeologists of the future are sifting through the rubble of my home, they will find millions of them.

*I will resist the urge to laugh myself silly at the idea that they will think the sheer quantity of these little metal sticks must mean that they hold a special significance.*

*Envy can be a positive motivator.*
*Let it inspire you to work harder*
*for what you want.*
— ROBERT BRINGLE

Browsing a knitting magazine at the library, I read of a knitter who had managed to procure some lace-weight cashmere. She wrote so compellingly about its legendary softness, its luminous color, and the pleasure she had working with it. She told of the heart-achingly beautiful wimple that she had knit from it, and how it was the envy of all the other knitters she knew, that it was simply the most beautiful wimple ever.

*I will realize that before I whip out the credit card and order myself a kit to make a cashmere wimple that I might want to take a minute and try to find out what the heck a wimple is.*

*Real success is finding your lifework
in the work that you love.*
— DAVID MCCULLOUGH

Most knitters can't imagine anything better than spending their days curled up knitting, shopping for wool, and getting paid for it.

*I will resist the urge to approach knitters in shops and ask them whether I can be their personal shopper, just so that I can spend somebody else's money on wool.*

# Frogging:

*the act of taking the knitting off the needles and pulling the working yarn to undo the stitches. This is done to unravel knitting completely or to pull the work out to a point before an error, when the knitting is replaced on needles. It is called "frogging" because you "rip-it, rip-it."*

It is important for knitters to know two things about frogging: that cats are capable of this knitting action, and even seem to enjoy it and seek opportunities to do it; and that foul language is a normal, healthy accompaniment to frogging, whether it is you or the cat that accomplished the task.

*I will allow myself the full expression of human frustration should I have to frog anything.*

*The future belongs to those who believe
in the beauty of their dreams.*

— MARIE CURIE

This is surely the motto of designers who work in knitted lace. It can only be faith alone that drives them, because, before it is stretched and blocked, lace in progress often resembles Chinese noodles.

*I will reserve judgment on my lace in progress until the magic of blocking has worked its charms.*

*It is not down in any map;*
*true places never are.*

— HERMAN MELVILLE

A portion of my stash is not for knitting; it is souvenir stash. The soft white wool that I bought in Newfoundland, the wool that I got in Hawaii (as an aside, this particular wool is probably worth keeping simply because I believe that it is the ONLY wool in Hawaii), the tweedy yarn my friend brought me from Ireland, the cotton from Italy. This is remembrance yarn. This yarn is not for knitting. With this yarn I can document every trip and yarn shop of my life. Who would knit that?

*I will remember that yarn can serve many purposes, and that it is possible non-knitters will never understand this.*

*The secret to creativity is knowing
how to hide your sources.*
— ALBERT EINSTEIN

The secret to storing lots of yarn is expanded thinking. There is really no reason why yarn cannot occupy any space not occupied by anything else. Take a fresh look at your home, closets, cupboards, and furniture, and ask yourself, "Can I fit a ball of yarn in here?" The world is suddenly full of possibilities. The liquor cabinet? Above books on the bookshelf? The freezer?

*I will think creatively before I decide that
I have run out of room for yarn.*

*Sometimes I get the feeling the whole world is against me, but deep down I know that's not true. Some smaller countries are neutral.*
— ROBERT ORBEN

5 ways to fix a mistake in your knitting:

1. Take the knitting off the needles and rip back the work, then put the work back on the needles.
2. Unknit the work, going back stitch by stitch.
3. If the mistake is near the bottom, cut the knitting, unravel it, put the work back on the needles, and knit back down again.
4. Cut only one stitch in the offending row, unknit those few stitches, repair them, and weave in the ends.
5. Light a small fire in a metal garbage can, and then throw the knitting in.

*I will remain open to drastic measures.*

*Ordinarily he was insane,*
*but he had lucid moments when*
*he was merely stupid.*
— HEINRICH HEINE

I have been trying to get my stash of yarn under control. My husband thinks this means that I am trying to get rid of some yarn. In truth, it actually means that I have been trying to find much, much better hiding spots.

*I will remember that there is more than one way to get control of an issue.*

*The first step towards amendment*
*is the recognition of error.*

— SENECA

Knitting patterns are notorious for having errors. It is a good practice to read through the pattern before you begin to see whether it seems right. If you run into trouble, you can check with the publisher or the Internet to find out whether an erratum for that pattern has been published. The very clever knitter will check for corrections to the pattern before beginning the project.

*Instead of spending 47 frustrating hours trying to figure out what I've done wrong and why I can't fix it while berating my knitting ability, I will consider the possibility that I'm not the one who screwed up.*

*If all else fails, immortality can always be assured by spectacular error.*
— JOHN KENNETH GALBRAITH

Many years ago, when I used to smoke, my lighter was often easier to find than my scissors. If I couldn't find the scissors, or was feeling too lazy to get up, I used the lighter to burn the yarn in one place to break it. Other than the smell, this worked fairly well. Later, when I found my scissors, I would cut off the little charred bits.

One day, I was knitting a cotton face-cloth and needed to cut the end. I flicked my lighter, expecting to singe the one spot, thus breaking the yarn.

*I will remember that cotton is highly flammable, and that the knitting Fates punish laziness. I will also remember that a flaming facecloth can be extinguished with a cup of coffee . . . in a pinch.*

*Make no little plans; they have no magic
to stir men's blood . . . Make big plans,
aim high in hope and work.*
— DANIEL H. BURNHAM

When I knit Fair Isle, I carry one color in my left and one in my right. This feat of hand-eye coordination is harder than zooming along with one color in my dominant hand. Give me Fair Isle and I knit each stitch more slowly, but each intriguing little row piles up on top of the other at an astonishing rate. With my wool as my witness, despite its apparent slowness, Fair Isle moves faster than plain knitting. Some say this is due to seeing the pattern emerge. It holds your interest and you work harder, enticing the image out of the wool.

I say it's the magic of Fair Isle.

*I will remember that, as unlikely as it seems, sometimes having the bravery to accept a knitting challenge is rewarded.*

You know you
knit too much when . . .

Your friends & family know
that you will always accept
yarn sight unseen. Garage
sale yarn, yarn from cleaned-
out basements, other knitters' castoffs, any yarn at all.

(All you ask is that they leave it
in a plain brown paper bag at the
door, because you like to pretend
you have a reputation to protect.)

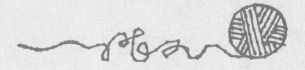

*You have to know how to accept rejection
and reject acceptance.*
— RAY BRADBURY

If you've knit for a three-year-old, then you understand. Just because he says he wants purple mittens, and you believe you have knit purple mittens, is no reason to believe that the three-year-old in question will believe that these are indeed purple mittens. It's a total crapshoot. As a general rule, I don't knit high investment items for toddlers. I stick to the small stuff. Hats are good. At least then, if you have spent a few weeks knitting a hat and then they dedicate their life to stuffing it behind the car seat and dropping it in the road, it doesn't sting like a spurned sweater.

*I will remember not to knit for three-year-olds unless I am going to be pretty relaxed about rejection.*

*I have found the best way to give advice to
your children is to find out what they
want and then advise them to do it.*
— HARRY S. TRUMAN

I have three daughters, and they all
know how to knit. The youngest
knits with persistence; the middle one
with a passion; and my eldest, now a
teenager, wouldn't be caught dead
with the needles in her hands. At first,
I thought it was because knitting wasn't
"hip enough" for her; then I thought
she was worried about what her friends
would think. Finally, I realized that
she doesn't knit . . . because I do.

*I will remember that kids need to rebel to
establish their own personalities, and that her
rejection of knitting is nothing personal. I will
also try not to rub it in when she takes it back
up in her twenties.*

*Our children seem to have wonderful taste,*
*or none — depending, of course,*
*on whether or not they agree with us.*
— ANONYMOUS

At my sister's request, I knit my nephew an acrylic hooded sweatshirt. I hated everything about it: the yarn, the pattern, the making up. With each moment and each stitch I cursed it. I swore on all I hold dear and all I believe to be true that I would never, ever knit its monotonous miles of stockinette stitch; its stupid, stupid pocket; its endless miles of I-cord ties; or its merciless, unending hood again.

Then I found out that my little nephew loves it, he wears it every day, and he is fast growing out of it.

*I will remember (as I cast on another acrylic hooded sweatshirt, in the next size) that I knit for love.*

*There is no reciprocity.*
*Men love women, women love children,*
*children love hamsters.*
— ALICE THOMAS ELLIS

If we could somehow magically gather up every hand-knit mitten ever lost by a child and put them in one place for reissue, I doubt seriously that anyone would ever need to knit another one.

*When knitting mittens for children, I will remember that they are inherently temporary. That no matter how elegant, stylish, or funky the mitten, children repel mittens on a biological level, and that the lack of respect for the mittens is not an indication of how little respect they have for the knitter.*

*Things won are done;*
*joy's soul lies in the doing.*
— WILLIAM SHAKESPEARE

I needed an easy project, something that I could work on while I watched TV or talked with my knitting friends. I picked a plain scarf with a plain yarn. I began to work with it and quickly discovered that the yarn split badly. It split so badly that I couldn't do anything else while I worked on it. It demanded my full attention for each stitch. I couldn't watch TV; I couldn't talk. After a little while, I discovered that this focused but simple knitting had its advantages. It was almost meditative to form plain stitch after plain stitch, watching the needles move hypnotically row after row.

*I will consider that paying attention to my knitting is a good thing, and probably what people are talking about when they say that knitting is "the new yoga."*

*Fashions fade, style is eternal.*
— YVES SAINT LAURENT

I've just finished knitting myself a copper and gold wrap, made from the most sparkly, elegant novelty yarn. Now, standing in front of the mirror with it draped oh so nonchalantly over my shoulders, I can imagine myself wearing it. I picture myself, tall and long-fingered, dangling a martini at a cocktail party, making witty conversation and charming everyone. The men are enchanted by me, and the women want to be me . . . and it's all because I knit myself a copper and gold evening wrap.

*I will try not to be too depressed when I realize how silly I'm going to look when I wear it to the only place my husband and I go these days — the grocery store.*

You know you
knit too much when ...

Your spouse likes to play a
little game with guests. He
calls it "What do you think
is in here?" and opens every
cupboard, chest, drawer, and
closet in the house to reveal
your yarn stash.

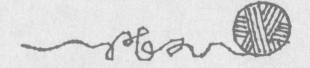

*No matter how cynical you get,*
*it is impossible to keep up.*
— LILY TOMLIN

Dear designer that I shall not name,

I recently purchased your knitting book
and was immediately struck by its artistic
merit. The photographs are so beautiful,
the models so stunning, and the settings
so authentic and breathtaking that I
scarcely even think of it as a book of
patterns, but rather, a tribute to the
skill and magnitude of your life's work.
I only have one question. I'd like to knit
the sweater on page 9, the one where
the model is turned toward the sunlight,
hair streaming down her back, but I'd
like to know whether that's a cardigan
or a pullover.

*I will tell designers that I would rather have
photos of sweaters that clearly show the details
of the garment than the incredible ability of
your photographer.*

*Ability is what you're capable of doing.*
*Motivation determines what you do.*
*Attitude determines how well you do it.*
— LOU HOLTZ

Gauge is a precision game; there is no room for a relaxed attitude. There are many knitters who, after knitting a couple of gauge swatches, make the classic error of thinking that a measly little inconsequential half stitch more per inch is no big deal. So it will be a little smaller. That's okay. For example, how about a sweater that has a bust measuring 40 inches, with a gauge of 4 stitches to 1 inch. You are getting 4½ stitches to the inch and you just ran out of patience for this whole "getting gauge game." You are planning to go ahead. In the end, you will end up with a sweater that is 35½ inches around. A half stitch in the other direction, and your sweater measures 46 inches. Gauge is serious business.

*I will remember that not everyone likes knitting to be serious. If I decide to play it fast and loose with gauge, I will make a point of befriending people of various sizes and shapes. It will fit someone.*

*We don't receive wisdom:*
*we must discover it for ourselves*
*after a journey that no one can*
*take for us or spare us.*
— MARCEL PROUST

As I carried the finished sweater to the bathtub for its "victory blocking," I practically danced. This sweater had been a big deal. It was fancy and complex and the pattern had stated the wrong amount of yarn and, despite getting gauge, I'd had to go back to the yarn shop twice to get more. I'd written the designer and she maintained that the yardage in the pattern was correct,

but somehow it had taken me an incredible six extra balls to finish it. I put
the sweater in the water to soak and
returned 10 minutes later. I lifted the
sweater from the water and just about
suffered a stroke. The sweater was huge.
Massive. Beyond colossal. The arms
dragged on the ground. I was heart-
broken; I couldn't even think of a
human it would fit.

*I will consider the possibility that, if it takes
me a great deal more yarn to knit something,
the extra yarn will surface at some point.*

*Under the fence,*
*Catch the sheep,*
*Back we come,*
*Off we leap!*

— A RHYME TO TEACH
   CHILDREN TO PURL

M any knitters hate purling because somebody told them that it was horrible.

*When I teach children to purl, I will make sure they don't get that idea from me, even if it means lying.*

*People who have what they want are fond
of telling people who haven't what they want
that they really don't want it.*
— OGDEN NASH

It is perhaps a sign that your attachment to your yarn (or yarn that you think should be yours, such as most of the stock in your local yarn shop) is getting out of hand if you have lied to another knitter about the properties of said yarn.

*In the interest of being a good and honest person, I will refrain from referring to the first-class merino in the shop as "scratchy" when I see someone else looking at it. There is butter that is scratchier than that yarn.*

*In through the front door,*
*Once around the back,*
*Peek through the window,*
*And off jumps Jack.*

— A RHYME TO TEACH
CHILDREN TO KNIT

I will remember that knitting is not hard, and that most children can learn to do it about the time they are ready to learn to read.

*I will remember, too, not to take it personally when they learn much faster than I did.*

You know you
knit too much when . . .

There is a knitting project
or yarn in every room of
your house, including the
bathroom.

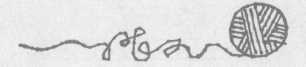

*Learning is not attained by chance,*
*it must be sought for with ardor*
*and attended to with diligence.*
— ABIGAIL ADAMS

My 11-year-old daughter was knitting the other day when she had a breakthrough, an accident that resulted in learning something incredible.

"Mom!" she said. "If you knit two together, you have one less stitch and you make the knitting smaller!"

"That's a good thing to know; that's a decrease," I replied, very, very impressed with my clever child. She had just made the same discovery that some other knitter had made for the first time in the fourth century. How many knitters have had this exact moment? Millions? Ladies-in-waiting, peasants in huts, lawyers in New York, nomads in the Arabian Desert. How many people down through history have thought, "Hey, if I knit two together . . ."

*I will stay connected to the history of knitting, while remembering that just because a billion people thought of this before my kid did, she's still freakin' brilliant.*

*We are hungry for things that
have touched human hands.*
— FAITH POPCORN

This is the reason that people are
driven to knit. This is why someone
will spend 59 hours making a sweater
when they could have had one that looks
like it for $20. This is why the words
"hand knit" are magical.

*I will remember, when I see a sweater in the
store just like the one I'm killing myself knitting, that even if mine turns out wonky and
crooked and costs me my sanity and more
money . . . I'm making a way better sweater.*

*A private railroad car is not*
*an acquired taste.*
*One takes to it immediately.*
— Eleanor R. Belmont

When I first started knitting, I used cheap acrylics. I was loath to spend my money on expensive yarns that my skills wouldn't live up to. Everything I knit was misshapen; the gauge was off; and my work was rife with dropped stitches, holes, and random increases and decreases.

When I was finally seduced by a fine wool, I was shocked by how quickly my work improved. Having good yarn to live up to was a powerful motivator.

*When choosing materials for my projects, I will buy the best that I can afford; there's not a lot of encouragement in cheap yarn.*

*Accept the challenges so that you can feel
the exhilaration of victory.*
— GEORGE S. PATTON

Knitters are driven by the challenge of taking a ball of string and turning it into a new and interesting finished object. This is what makes knitting a pair of socks or mittens a double dare. Halfway through, you are confused by the presence of a completely finished garment.

*I will accept that things that come in pairs are a unique opportunity for a knitter to prove her tenacity and rise to a challenge. I will also accept that if I know someone who is willing to wear mismatched socks, I may never meet this challenge.*

# Tinking:

*the act of unknitting knitting
one stitch at a time.*

It is used to correct small and recent errors, and its advantage is that the knitting need not be removed from the needles, saving time and concern for dropped stitches. It is called "tink" because that is "knit" spelled backward.

*I will consider, no matter how afraid I am that I might not be able to get my work back on the needles, that tinking is not the answer if I need to undo 67 rows of 100 stitches.*

*A positive attitude may not solve all*
*your problems, but it will annoy enough*
*people to make it worth the effort.*
— HERM ALBRIGHT

There are many different ways to knit socks. I use the flap heel, always, every time. I think it's pretty clever, I like that I can reinforce the flap where the back of the shoe rubs, and I like picking up stitches for the gussets. I lied. I *love* picking up stitches for the gussets. I like that, at least in my mind, when I turn the heel, I am halfway. Gloriously halfway.

*When celebrating the halfway point on a sock, I will try to let my joy be complete, and forget that there is still another sock to go.*

*Hard work never killed anybody,*
*but why take a chance?*
— EDGAR BERGEN

Intarsia is pretty cool, but its downside is that when you are finished there are a multitude of ends to weave in. We all wish there was some way around this but, sadly, there is no way to do intarsia without ends decorating the inside like shag carpet. I would advise you to weave in as you go . . . as I've learned from my mistakes. The last time I did intarsia, when I left all the ends until I was finished, then, overwhelmed by the sheer mass of ends, I suffered a fit of apoplexy and denied all knowledge of the sweater.

*I will remember that weaving in as I go increases the odds of having a finished project.*

*Just think of all those women on the*
*Titanic who said, "No, thank you,"*
*to dessert that night. And for what!*
— ERMA BOMBECK

When I was frustrated that my baby daughter wouldn't sleep through the night, my mother urged me to be patient. "This could be the last night she gets up," she told me. "How do you want your last nighttime feeding to be?" I've applied this attitude to my yarn-buying activity. This could be the last yarn I buy. What would I want the last yarn I buy to be? What if tomorrow . . . I can't buy yarn anymore?

*I will remember that this attitude, although it increases the quality of yarn that I buy and my willingness to treat myself, can hamper my ability to pay the mortgage.*

*There are no menial jobs,*
*only menial attitudes.*

— WILLIAM BENNETT

Once you get the hang of them, socks can be pretty mundane. A plain navy blue dress sock for my husband goes around and around and around enough times that I begin to imagine that grooming a llama with my tongue would be more fun. I play little games with myself, races to see how fast I can knit, bribing myself with coffee or chocolate at the end of each row . . . but, to be quite honest, a navy blue dress sock is an insult to the knitter, and this is elevated to injury when you realize you still have to knit a second one.

*When considering this menial task, I will remember that my husband puts "she knits me dress socks" at the top of the list when he recounts the reasons that he loves me.*

*Put duties aside at least an hour before bed and perform soothing, quiet activities that will help you relax.*
— DIANNE HALES

Knitting is perfect for this. I make a habit of setting aside some time each evening to take out my knitting and work quietly on it, happily relaxing. I believe that it prepares me for sleep and washes away the cares of my day.

*I will consider that intarsia, or Fair Isle with three or more colors in a row, prepares nobody for sleep and cursing loudly while flinging knitting around the living room is about as far away from soothing as you can get.*

*Lack of money is the root of all evil.*
— George Bernard Shaw

If I were going to shoplift something (not that I ever would, of course), it would be lace-weight Shetland wool.

Many yards is still a skein small enough to fit in a pocket, it is exquisite, and it is expensive. The perfect crime.

*I will remember, the next time I hear that someone has been charged with theft, to extend my sympathy and try to find understanding. After all, maybe she stole wool.*

*A successful marriage requires*
*falling in love many times,*
*always with the same person.*
— MIGNON MCLAUGHLIN

I am happily married to a wonderful man, who is generous, funny, and kind. I have never even for one moment contemplated leaving him or being unfaithful. At least, that was true until I found out that one of the women in our knitting guild is married to a man who owns a yarn store and builds her cedar-lined, moth-repelling closets as his hobby.

I can't stop thinking about him.

*I will remember (in the midst of an obsession with a man I've never met) that my husband has his own special qualities.*

You know you
knit too much when ...

Your knitting children have
accused you (openly, and
more than once) of giving
them only your "crap wool"
for their projects.

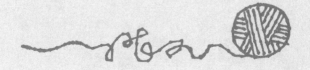

*I detest converts almost as much*
*as I do missionaries.*

— H. L. MENCKEN

One night, as I sat knitting in a restaurant after the movies, the waitress asked a few questions about my project. Next thing I knew, she was sitting at the table with needles in her hands.

When she had gone back to her work, my husband asked me whether this was what it had come to. "What?" I asked.

"Missionary work," he replied.

*I will remember that spreading the word of wool around the world is a good thing, and that many, many people want to learn to knit. I will also remember that if they start looking nervously at the exit I may have taken it too far.*

*The universe is full of magical things,*
*patiently waiting for our wits to grow sharper.*
— EDEN PHILLPOTTS

There are many ancient stories of knitting, and there are even some that tell of knitting as a magic charm — spells that can be wrought in the stitches of sweaters, blankets, and socks for purposes known only to the knitter. One of these stories recounts how knitters used to knit a hair from their own locks into the garment for another, thus binding that person to them forever.

*I will accept the legend of this magic charm, both because it is lovely and because it is easier to believe in magic than to try and pick my hair out of my knitting all the time.*

# NONIA:

*Newfoundland Outport Nursing and
Industrial Association*

In 1920, there was a shortage of doctors, nurses, and midwives in the isolated outports of Newfoundland, Canada. The British government sent over some nurses but, as is often the way with governments, the funding for this health service was touch and go. The nurses came up with the idea that if they were to knit items to sell, they could fund the program themselves. They recruited women from all over Newfoundland, gave them wool, and taught them to knit (if they didn't know already). The women knit what pleased them, and NONIA picked up the knitting, paid the women, and then sold the knitting to pay for more health care. It was without a doubt one of the cleverest women-helping-women schemes ever thought up. The nurses kept their jobs, the women earned a little income, and everybody in the outports got health care.

*I will remember that knitting can be a powerful force for helping others.*

*The only difference between me and
a madman is that I'm not mad.*
— SALVADOR DALÌ

There are knitters in the world who work in miniature. They use needles made from piano wire, and their gauge averages about 40 to 60 stitches to the inch. Yeah, read that again.

*I will remember, though I have absolutely no urge to take up this type of endeavor, that it does give some perspective to complaining about projects in fingering-weight yarn.*

*And isn't sanity really just a one-trick pony,*
*anyway? I mean, all you get is one trick,*
*rational thinking. But when you're good and*
*crazy, ooh ooh ooh, the sky's the limit!*
— THE TICK (BEN EDLUND)

Artist and performer Pate Conaway worked on a performance piece called "Knitting for My Soul." He knitted in public, a washcloth sculpture that would cover a queen-size bed. His needles were 4 feet long, and the ball of yarn was almost as big as he was. Pate claimed to be playing with scale.

*I will follow my inner artist as far as she*
*wants to take me. (Even if it's not quite*
*that far.)*

*For people allergic to wool,*
*one's heart can only bleed.*
— ELIZABETH ZIMMERMAN

5 reasons why wool is wonderful:

1. It can be bent 20,000 times without breaking
2. It is warm even when wet
3. It is fire resistant; wool will stop burning when the flame is removed
4. It can be stretched up to 30 percent and still return to its original shape
5. Sheep are easier to catch and shear than, say, musk ox

*Once is happenstance.*
*Twice is coincidence.*
*Three times is enemy action.*
— IAN L. FLEMING

My sweater is against me. I have no real proof, of course, because sweaters are tricky, but it is the only possibility. I know people will think that a sweater plagued with mistakes and disaster is my fault . . . but I am a competent knitter who has a closet full of sweaters that went just fine. Clearly, I am not to blame for the dropped stitches, the funny gauge, and the cable that went the wrong way.

*I will remember, when a project is not going my way, that everything on the planet has its own destiny. From time to time, I need to accept that my project and I are not on the same "life path."*

*I'm living so far beyond my income*
*that we may almost be said*
*to be living apart.*

— E. E. CUMMINGS

One strategy for controlling your spending at the yarn shop is to decide how much money you will spend before you leave your house. Take that amount of cash and leave your credit cards at home. Temptation will be everywhere when you are at the yarn shop, and your self-control will be tested. This simple technique can reduce impulse shopping and help you stay focused.

*When I run out of cash, I will simply take my yarn and go home, instead of trying to sell my shoes and coat on the street in front of the yarn shop to raise more funds.*

*Knitting still remains my most stimulating yet relaxing activity and I thank the powers that be that I can make a living at it . . . I always pack my knitting or needlepoint project first when traveling.*

— KAFFE FASSETT

For most knitters, traveling means scoring some really good knitting time, but what project to take? Travel knitting must be small, but not so small that you would finish it quickly and need a new project. Simple enough to amuse you, but not so simple that you will be bored. The yarn should be lightweight so that you can carry all you will need. It must suit the climate; you don't want to take a wool sweater to the beach or a sunhat to the Arctic . . . and finally, it must be washable so you can get your spilled margarita off it.

*I will remember that it's normal for it to take longer to pack my knitting than my clothes.*

*Just because something doesn't do*
*what you planned it to do*
*doesn't mean it's useless.*
— THOMAS A. EDISON

Unaware that I was headed for likely disaster, I knit my friend a pair of slippers that needed to be felted. I used leftovers in my stash and knit the tops out of red yarn from one company and black yarn of a different brand. When I took them out of the washer I was stunned. The red wool had shrunk at a completely different rate than the black. The slippers were round and flat, and they bore no resemblance to the foot of any mammal on Earth.

*Remember to think inventively. I may not have made slippers, but I did have wool Frisbees, or some really interesting hot pads.*

*Really, all you need to become
a good knitter are wool, needles, hands,
and slightly below-average intelligence.
Of course, superior intelligence, such as
yours and mine, is an advantage.*
— ELIZABETH ZIMMERMAN

There is nothing like working out a piece of knitting to make you feel intelligent. Of course, there's nothing quite like getting your superior intelligence kicked by a piece of yarn and two needles to let the air right out of that self-confidence.

*I will remember to be humble, even when I am knitting cleverly. Things change.*

*He who works with his hands is a laborer,*
*he who works with his hands and his head*
*is a craftsman, he who works with his hands,*
*his head and his heart is an artist.*
— FRANCIS OF ASSISI

# My definitions:

**Craft Knitting** — knitting a sweater from someone else's pattern but making changes in the yarn and style to suit your taste.

**Art Knitting** — knitting a sweater from any pattern, but altering the pattern, stitch, or colorway to make it completely your own.

**Labor Knitting** — knitting a sweater with a 50-inch chest.

*I will not allow anyone else (including this book) to tell me when I am making art.*

*Problems worthy of attack prove their*
*worth by fighting back.*
— PAUL ERDOS

Some knitters use a "lifeline" when knitting complex patterns. They thread a strand of waste yarn through a row of stitches that they know is correct, and then continue on. This maneuver is repeated at regular intervals. If a mistake is discovered, the work can be ripped back to the lifeline, and the stitches held by it picked up and the work resumed.

Then there are those of us who laugh in the face of danger and call these knitters "chicken."

*Should I choose to enjoy "daredevil" knitting and scorn a lifeline, I will gracefully accept the consequences, or at least give up mocking more cautious knitters when the decision comes back to haunt me.*

*There is no right way to knit; there is
no wrong way to knit. So if anybody kindly
tells you that what you are doing is "wrong,"
don't take umbrage; they mean well.
Smile submissively, and listen, keeping your
disagreement on an entirely mental level.*
— ELIZABETH ZIMMERMAN

If you knit long enough, you will discover that no matter what your style or expertise is, there is another "expert" who is convinced you are doing it wrong. She will believe this despite the fact that you are both producing beautiful knitting.

*I will remember that individuality is a good thing, in life and in knitting.*

*One cannot collect all the beautiful shells*
*on the beach. One can collect only a few,*
*and they are more beautiful if they are few.*
— ANNE MORROW LINDBERGH

This is one theory of yarn buying. We must not overburden ourselves with greed and want, but instead gather only a few . . . just those perfect balls of yarn that are special to us. Limiting the amount of yarn that we stash makes us treasure those few balls even more, and it ensures that we actually fulfill the destiny of those meager skeins.

*This works fine if you think "a few" should be followed by the word "hundred."*

*If everything seems to be going well,*
*you have obviously overlooked something.*
— STEVEN WRIGHT

Excellent, I have just carefully worked the armhole decreases on the front of the sweater. I'm feeling pretty good about myself. It was tricky; I had to really work to incorporate the cables into the decreases, but I persevered and I'm ready for the next instruction. I look at the pattern and my heart sinks as I read "at the same time" followed by the directions for the neck shaping that I was to have done.

*It is not a waste of time to read ahead in the pattern; most sweaters need necks.*

*Failing to plan is planning to fail.*
— ALAN LAKEIN

If you are using a pattern with multiple sizes it is a good idea to circle, highlight, or otherwise mark the instructions for the size you are knitting. There is very little comfort for the knitter who has knit a sweater with a size small front and a size large back.

*You are excused from this rule if you know a small-chested hunchback you could give the sweater to.*

*The cure for boredom is curiosity.*
*There is no cure for curiosity.*
— ELLEN PARR

3 ways to liven up a yarn shop:

- Loudly, and in a clear voice, say, "Circular needles are so stupid."
- Wait until the shop is crowded, then tell one person that today is the day that everything is 50 percent off.
- Yell "MOTH!"

*Not that you could be bored in a yarn shop, but just in case.*

> *Do not trust your memory;*
> *it is a net full of holes; the most*
> *beautiful prizes slip through it.*
> — GEORGES DUHAMEL

A few years ago, when I ran out of space for yarn, I started tucking it away, a ball here and there. A skein of silk in the gravy boat, some tweed down the sleeves of an unused coat, a whole sweater's worth in the canning pot I rarely used. I feel clever, and now I have room for way more.

*I'm looking forward to getting older. As my memory fails me, I will get the pleasure of finding it all again.*

*Planning is an unnatural process;*
*it is much more fun to do something.*
*The nicest thing about not planning is*
*that failure comes as a complete surprise,*
*rather than being preceded by a period*
*of worry and depression.*
— Sir John Harvey-Jones

I needed to cut steeks in my Fair Isle sweater and was perhaps overplanning and overconcerned. I realized that I'd slipped over the edge when I heard my daughter inviting over a friend.

"Hey, do you want to come over? My mom's supposed to cut up this sweater and she's really freaking out."

*Sometimes you need to cut steeks quickly, before you become "entertainment" for the whole neighborhood.*

*The only really good place to buy lumber is at a store where the lumber has already been cut and attached together in the form of furniture, finished, and put inside boxes.*
— DAVE BARRY

I overheard my husband telling some friends that I was not very "handy" and that the words "some assembly required" were sure trouble. Although I agree that the bookshelf incident last year was pretty ugly, I still think he's wrong.

*I'm a knitter. My projects are the ultimate in "some assembly required."*

*A work of art is above all*
*an adventure of the mind.*
— EUGÈNE IONESCO

I know this will come as a shock to some of you, but knitting is a bit of a gamble. It is possible that you can knit a swatch, wash and measure it, carefully calculate your gauge, absolutely study a pattern, execute it with patience and perfection . . . and still end up with something unexpected. This element of risk is what keeps the more adventurous of us knitting.

*I will try to stay connected to my cheerful sense of adventure the next time an absolutely perfect sweater grows by 3 feet the first time I wear it.*

*Though we travel the world over to
find the beautiful, we must carry it
with us or we find it not.*
— RALPH WALDO EMERSON

Before I leave home on a trip, I plan
to see all the significant things about
the location I'm traveling to. I want to
make sure I see everything I can. I do
research and note all the places I want
to see: places of worship, historical land-
marks, natural wonders, and yarn shops.

*I will resist the voice in my head that says
there's no point in traveling to an incredible
European village just because they don't sell
wool there.*

*I saw the angel in the marble and
carved until I set him free.*
— MICHELANGELO

Some knitters purchase yarn with a pattern and a plan. They buy with a specific goal, and most of it is used more or less immediately and as planned. Others talk about the yarn "telling them what it wants to be." They buy and hoard yarns, seemingly at random, until a yarn speaks to them about its destiny. There is sometimes a lag of 20 years or more between a yarn purchase and its realization as a knitted item, although there may be several periods of swatching and "false starts." This process cannot be rushed, or failure is certain.

*Both ways are good, but if you prefer the latter, you need way more closet space.*

*True art is characterized by an irresistible urge in the creative artist.*
— ALBERT EINSTEIN

Sometimes I just stare at my husband. He has lived with a knitter all these years and yet has seemingly learned nothing of our ways. He is still able to say the most ridiculous things about knitting. For example, just the other day I was showing him some beautiful blue yarn in a catalog. He actually looked at the yarn (which was 80 percent wool and 20 percent mohair) and said to me, "Don't you already have blue yarn in the stash just like that?"

I could scarcely believe it. The blue yarn in the stash is 70 percent wool and 30 percent mohair. He has no idea.

*I'm so misunderstood as an artist.*

*Knitting, Knitting, 1, 2, 3,*
*I knit the scarves for Roo and me;*
*I love honey and I love tea;*
*Knitting, Knitting, 1, 2, 3.*
— KATHLEEN W. ZOEHFELD

When my mother learned that she was pregnant with me, she decided that she should learn to knit. She started with a simple yellow scarf and worked on it (and hated it) until I was born. With each successive pregnancy my mom hauled out the poor yellow scarf, and with each baby it grew by an inch or two.

By the time my mother was having her fourth baby, I was five, and my grandmother had taught me to knit while my poor mother was still working on the yellow scarf. My grandmother came to visit one day and saw the scarf on the table. She picked it up and examined the stitches, then remarked (obviously thinking it was my work), "Well, now, that's not bad for a five-year-old." Mortified, my mother picked up the scarf and dropped it in the garbage.

*She has never knit again. She doesn't mind.*

You know you
knit too much when . . .

Your non-knitting spouse
starts trying to feign interest
in your knitting, just so that
you will talk to him, saying
things such as, "So, are we
knitting or purling?" or,
"So how do you really feel
about cables?"

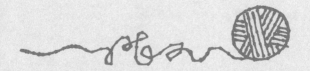

*Geographically, Ireland is a medium-sized*
*rural island that is slowly but steadily*
*being consumed by sheep.*
— DAVE BARRY

It is likely a unique hallmark of knitters that they don't think of a country being consumed by sheep, but rather a country that is being converted to wool.

*I will recognize that it is another unique hallmark of being a knitter that this quotation alone, without knowing anything else about the country, is enough to make me want a plane ticket to Ireland.*

*What Heracles said is true, O Argonauts!*
*On the Quest of the Golden Fleece*
*our lives and our honors depend.*
*To Colchis — to Colchis must we go!*

— PADRAIC COLUM,
*The Golden Fleece and the*
*Heroes Who Lived Before Achilles*

In the Greek myth of Jason and the Argonauts, Jason embarks on a heroic quest to find and retrieve the Golden Fleece. Although most of the events are rooted in mythos, the Golden Fleece itself has a historical explanation. In the Colchis region of Greece, people used to pan for gold using, you guessed it, a sheep's fleece. The fleece was held under running water, such as a stream, and the little bits of gold would be caught in it. If you had a very successful day, you would have "a golden fleece."

*I will try to stop thinking about what a cute evening top I could knit out of the spectacular golden yarn.*

*The telephone is a good way to talk to people without having to offer them a drink.*
— FRAN LEBOWITZ

For quite some time I've been trying to work out a really good way to knit while I'm on the phone. Right now I'm simply clenching the phone between my shoulder and head, but I make more mistakes when I'm looking at my knitting sideways. I also suspect that this practice is probably the cause of the weird muscle spasm I've developed that keeps suddenly and randomly twisting my head at a 45-degree angle while I'm doing other things.

*I will recognize that it is not normal to think that the bigger problem in this picture is the mistakes in my knitting, rather than the permanent inability to hold my head straight.*

*Arguments are to be avoided; they are
always vulgar and often convincing.*
— OSCAR WILDE

Here's a hypothetical question. If a knitter (not me, you understand) and her mate were to suddenly find themselves with more money than they were expecting, and they were discussing how best this windfall could be spent, and the knitter's husband (not my husband, of course) had made several good points about the future, and the future of the children, would said husband be entitled to accuse the knitter in question of being "selfish" and "out of her mind" (even though the knitter makes many, many lovely knitted things for this husband and children, and hardly anything, ever, for herself) if she were to suggest that the largest part of the sum be spent on yarn?

*I didn't think so.*

You know you
knit too much when . . .

You get your income tax
refund in the mail and,
despite owning almost as
much as a modest yarn shop,
you and your mate begin
immediate negotiations to
determine what portion
of it will be spent on wool.

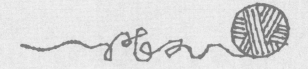

*The price is what you pay;*
*the value is what you receive.*

— ANONYMOUS

The frugal knitter will quickly develop a taste for fine wool on tiny needles. There are many, many yards in those wee balls, and it take lots and lots of tiny stitches to make anything. One hundred grams of chunky wool lasts only a few hours, but 100 grams of fingering-weight wool takes a good long time to knit up.

*I will balance my cheapskate desire to get maximum knitting time for the dollar with my desire to retain my eyesight.*

*A baby is an inestimable blessing and bother.*
— MARK TWAIN

The head of a newborn baby only appears petite and charming. Baby heads are actually really big. (Ask whoever gave birth to the baby in question.) Many knitters make the mistake of knitting a sweet little neck on baby sweaters. After years of disappointment (and near stranglings), I have finally come up with a strategy to get them right. First, knit a neck that is so big that it can't possibly be right. You will know you are close to the first stage when you think to yourself, "that's too big for sure." Now add 10 percent. Then cast off very, very loosely.

*I will resist the urge to swear off childbearing and stop advising others to avoid it as well when I have to rip back this neck and add a slit and buttons to get the newborn baby's head through.*

*Nothing astonishes men so much as
common sense and plain dealing.*
— Ralph Waldo Emerson

Last night while I was knitting I had a great idea. Stay with me, it's a radical idea, and I wouldn't want to shock anyone. What if, somehow, we had just one system of measurement for knitting needles? Would it really be so crazy if the needle I'm holding couldn't be a 4mm, a #8 Imperial, or a #6 US, but just one of those three? What if I knew that the pattern I was reading referred only to that size, and it didn't leave me trying to figure out which needle to use based on the country that the pattern was published in. I say we need a petition.

*When I am finished organizing the world's system of knitting needle measurement, I will turn my attention to the equally stupid system for screwdrivers. (Do there really need to be so many kinds?)*

*A friend is a second self.*

— ARISTOTLE

There is nothing that does a knitter's heart more good than finding a dear, dear friend who knits. There is very little that is more fun than sitting with someone who loves you, laughs at your jokes, and truly wants to have a two-hour conversation on the revelation you had about twisted ribbing.

*I will keep in mind, should I be blessed enough to find a darling friend who loves knitting as much as I do, that if we go to a yarn shop together I shouldn't knock her down like we have never even met when I see mohair on sale.*

*When your hobbies get in the way*
*of your work — that's okay;*
*but when your hobbies get in the way*
*of themselves . . . well . . .*
— STEVE MARTIN

As I go sneaking up the aisle of the darkened movie theatre, I reflect that I love knitting. What other hobby can you do at the movies? Passing into the lobby, I notice an odd noise is following me, but before I can investigate, I'm suddenly on the floor, yarn wrapped around my foot. A glance back down the aisle reveals that some moron has dragged knitting up the entire length of the theatre, before it got stuck in the lobby door. Worse, that moron has left a trail of tangled yarn that leads clearly back to my seat. I endure the snickers and stares of the entire left side of the theater as I wind the yarn back up every long step of the aisle.

*Movies are prime knitting time. Take simple work you don't need to look at; use wooden needles, so the noise doesn't bother anyone; and for goodness sake, put your knitting away carefully before you go to the restroom.*

# WHACO:
## *Wool Housing and Containment Overflow*

Many knitters suffer from this common ailment, although complaints tend to be registered more often by those living with knitters. Symptoms include wool sprouting from drawers intended to hold other things, bookshelves with yarn and books alternating in disarray, and a tendency for one's stash to burst suddenly from closets. Affected knitters also continue to purchase yarn, often at a frightening rate, despite the absolute lack of anywhere to keep it.

Treatment involves . . . well, nobody has ever successfully treated it, as victims can only rarely be convinced that this much yarn is a "problem."

*Should I fall victim to WHACO, I will appreciate that it is easier to convince my family that it requires no treatment if I can find just one wool-free room to sit in.*

*The ability to simplify means to
eliminate the unnecessary so that
the necessary may speak.*
— HANS HOFMANN

From time to time (well, fairly often, actually), a knitter gets her nose out of joint when a knitted gift isn't appreciated. There is a tendency among the non-knitting to underestimate the time and expense involved in a hand-knit hat. It's understandable. How could they know? I suggest the following: from now on, using your stitch and row gauge and the size of the finished item, calculate the approximate number of stitches that you knit to create the item.

*I can appreciate that a tag reading "These socks contain 20,000 stitches, each lovingly handmade" would shut up Uncle Bob pretty quick.*

*The beginning is the most important*
*part of the work.*

— PLATO

There are about 30 ways to cast on in knitting. Long tail, provisional, cable, crochet, backward loop . . . the mind reels. They all have their merits. Some are solid, some are stretchy, some leave you ready to work a right-side row, and some look better with ribbing. The wise knitter learns several and uses each to its best advantage.

*I accept that even though there are myriad possibilities for casting on, somehow for each pattern there is still only one right number to cast on.*

*Like religion, politics, and family planning,*
*cereal is not a topic to be brought up in*
*public. It's too controversial.*
— ERMA BOMBECK

There rages a debate between those who admire acrylic yarns, citing durability, washability and nonscratchiness, and those who fall firmly in the wool camp. They cite the warmth and softness of wool and the pleasure of working with something that comes from the natural world. I have learned that this subject is too volatile to bring up in public, as the conversation can end with hurt feelings and phrases such as "yarn snob" being bandied about, no matter which yarn you profess to prefer.

*I can promise, in the interest of peace, that if I ever divulge a fellow knitter's fiber choice, I will immediately follow it with the statement "Not that there's anything wrong with that."*

*An expert is a person who has made
all the mistakes that can be made in
a very narrow field.*

— Niels Bohr

I knew a woman who had been knitting for more than 65 years, and I, in the infancy of my serious knitting obsession, was looking for a mentor. I figured that this woman would be perfect; she was kind and patient and had to know everything there was to know about knitting. I was absolutely shocked to discover that she knew very little about the world of knitting. She knew one cast on, one cast off, one way to increase, and one way to decrease. She knew them better than anyone had ever known them, but her experience was limited. I realized that she had been using the same few techniques and patterns her whole life. Despite her age and experience, she was not an "expert," except at her own few techniques.

*I will realize that it is a knitter's willingness to try new things and make mistakes that creates an "expert," not just the years of experience.*

*A man is not idle because he is absorbed
in thought. There is visible labor and
there is invisible labor.*

— VICTOR HUGO

I know knitters who feel guilty for sitting and knitting when they should be "working." What, I ask you, about knitting does not qualify as work? It is productive, it is thrifty, it is creating useful items for fellow humans, and it is a thoughtful and enlightening use of the intellect. True, it's not as exciting as doing the laundry, but really, what is?

*Should I feel pangs of guilt, I will remember that just because something is fun doesn't mean it's a waste of time.*

You know you
knit too much when . . .

You seek out forms of
exercise that you can do
while knitting, such as
riding a stationary bike.

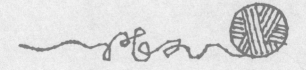

*Out of the strain of the Doing,*
*Into the peace of the Done.*
— JULIA LOUISE WOODRUFF

There is nothing I can tell the non-knitter that explains the joy of a finished object. Running your hands over a beautiful sweater that you, yourself changed from useless yarn to a lovely garment with two pointed sticks and your cleverness . . . it's like knowing a fancy magic trick. It's an homage to your intelligence and patience and a moment of real and profound pride.

*Even though I am very excited that I have finished this sweater, I will resist the urge to go next door and show it to my neighbors. Last time they weren't as impressed as I thought they would be.*

*To save time, take time to check gauge.*
— EVERY KNITTING PATTERN
EVER WRITTEN

There are those knitters who believe that gauge is a vital component of knitting. They take time to check it at the beginning of every project, and they have a stack of swatches to prove it. For their diligence they are rewarded with garments of predictable size and shape. Then there are the rest of us, who occasionally take risks with gauge, neglect swatches, and live on the edge. For our lack of diligence, we are credited with inventing the "cowl neck" sweater.

*If I neglect gauge, I will gracefully accept the consequences.*

You know you
knit too much when . . .

Your friends, who cheerfully
used to call you an "enabler"
when you encouraged them
to purchase yarn, have
started calling you a
"pusher."

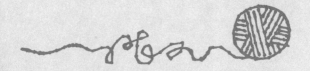

*Let's have some new clichés.*
— Samuel Goldwyn

Despite what we knitters know to be true, the non-knitting world somehow persists in thinking that a "knitter" looks a certain way. Most likely, this picture is one of an elderly woman, grandmotherly and polite, sitting in her rocking chair surrounded by homemade cookies and accompanied by a certain number of cats.

In reality, a knitter today is just as likely to be young, hip, male, and sitting at a "Stitch and Bitch" in a local bar. Several of today's best knitting designers are men, and a knitter is as likely to have body piercings as homemade cookies.

*Despite our diversity, the tendency to be accompanied by a cat is an oddity among knitters that cannot be explained.*

*Friends don't let friends knit drunk.*
— ANONYMOUS

When I was in college, there was a knitting club. I went a couple of times but quickly learned a valuable lesson. The club met in the university pub, and after a couple of episodes of drinking and knitting, I quickly realized that this was not the combination for me. Not that I didn't have a good time; it was great. It was simply that the hangover made correcting my wild drunken mistakes too painful to contemplate. The result was always two days of lost knitting time.

*Should the temptation to knit at a party or pub overwhelm me with ideas of camaraderie and candlelight knitting, I will either order a soft drink or stick to garter stitch.*

*Ideas are the factors that lift civilization.*
*They create revolutions. There is more*
*dynamite in an idea than in many bombs.*
— BISHOP VINCENT

How grateful are we to the first person to think, "Hey, you know what would be a good idea? If we all didn't have to spin our own yarn. What if I invented a machine that would spin it for me? Then I could make enough to be able to sell it to people who just wanted to knit!"

*I can remember to think kindly of the inventions and inventors who made it so that I can just go to the yarn shop instead of wrestling a full-grown angry sheep to the ground holding shears in my teeth.*

*Hide not your talents, they for use were made.*
*What's a sundial in the shade?*
— BENJAMIN FRANKLIN

How many times have you diminished knitting? Someone praised your work and you said, "Oh, it was nothing." (Yeah, nothing. Sixty-seven hours knitting a cabled afghan, squinting into the dark wool and muttering suspicious things . . . nothing.) Or how about, "No, no . . . it was easy." (Easy? Do you normally use foul language in the presence of decent upstanding wool? Normally have a twitch over your eye? Normally stay up late into the night just to finish one more row?) From now on I am telling the truth. I'm taking back knitting as a respectable art, one to be contended with.

*The next time your knitting is complimented, raise your needles and repeat after me: "Thank you. It was a challenge, but I did it."*

*I have learned to use the word 'impossible'*
*with the greatest caution.*
— WERNHER VON BRAUN

Barb Hunt uses knitting to create replicas of antipersonnel land mines to raise awareness. Debbie New has knitted a boat and a grandfather clock. Janet Morton made a balaclava for a rhinoceros, a cardigan for a giraffe, and a remarkable "house cozy" that covered an entire cottage on Toronto Island, dressing the house for winter.

*I have personally knit an Aran sweater for a 6'4" man with a 48-inch chest. Nothing is impossible.*

You know you
knit too much when . . .

You have ordered in pizza
for dinner so you can have
more knitting time, even
though you don't really
like pizza. Double points
if you have done it twice
in one week.

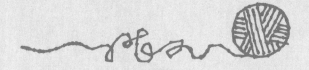

*Out of the mouths of babes . . .*

— PSALMS 8:2

After several painstaking hours of teaching my youngest to knit, during which her patience with me was sorely tested, and I wondered why on earth I was trying to share this with her when she appeared not yet ready for the pleasures of knitting, my five-year-old finally warmed my heart by saying, "Hey, Mom, guess what? Knitting is fun!"

*I will consider, during the less-than-rewarding phase of teaching a child to knit, that if I impale myself on my knitting needles I will miss hearing a very great truth.*

*Silence is the most perfect expression of scorn.*
— GEORGE BERNARD SHAW

My kids claim that there is a kind of knitting I do that they call "angry knitting." They say that they can come into a room, look at the way I am knitting, and know that something has pushed me close to losing my temper.

I know this is nonsense. I am an expert knitter, and I do not let my emotions alter my knitting style. I am eternal and unchangeable, and I am sure that there is no more "angry knitting" than there is "tender knitting."

*I am willing to consider that my emotions may affect my knitting, now that I have discovered the sleeve I worked the night my daughter came in late is so tightly knit that it easily measures 3 inches narrower than the other.*

*With great power comes great responsibility.*
— UNCLE BEN PARKER,
from Marvel's comic *Spider-man*

I find, as I know many other knitters do, mistakes in a knitting pattern to be unbearable. Designers hold our precious knitting time in their hands, and there is nothing that can be done to make it up to a knitter who has just spent 57 excruciating hours questioning her own sanity and ability, developing a tic, and cursing at the cat, while ripping her yarn threadbare trying to knit something that has an error in the pattern.

*When I run the world, test-knitting a pattern before selling it will be law. I'm not sure what the punishment for breaking this law will be, but it will take at least 57 hours.*

*My theory is that men are no more liberated than women.*
— INDIRA GANDHI

I was teaching a children's knitting class in the rear of a toy shop. Halfway through class a little boy shopping with his mother wandered over and approached an 11-year-old boy happily and expertly knitting a potholder.

"Hey!" he laughed, "boys don't knit!" "Clearly," said the manly young knitter, "they do."

*I will take care not to pass on any gender biases I may have to the next generation.*

*Generosity is giving more than you can,*
*and pride is taking in less than you need.*
— KAHLIL GIBRAN

Knitting for charity is a lovely, lovely thing. There are knitters who knit hats for preemies, warm clothing for children, pads for animal shelters, blankets for the war-torn, chemo caps for cancer patients, and many, many more. The generous knitter can find a multitude of ways to turn her knitting into a good deed. I want to make a difference in the world, too, and I've tried knitting for charity. That said, when after six months I had knit only a hat and a blanket square, I realized that a charity may need my yarn money more than my slow knitting.

*Should I be unable to knit fast enough or often enough to make a difference with my knitting, I will remember that most charities could really use my time and money, too.*

You know you
knit too much when . . .

You hear about a breed of
"miniature sheep" that
grow to be only 16 inches
in height and weigh only
50 pounds, and immediately
start trying to figure out
whether you can convince
your spouse it's a dog.

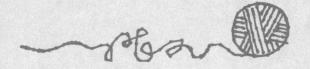

*You'll find boredom where there is*
*the absence of a good idea.*
— EARL NIGHTINGALE

Knitting is a boon for those of us who are easily bored. I take my knitting everywhere to take the edge off of moments that would otherwise drive me stark raving mad. Waiting in line, waiting for appointments, waiting for lectures or meetings to begin. Knitting adds interest to even the most tedious and mundane moments.

*I will remember, because I am not the only one who has figured this out, that it might be offensive to knit while I am out to dinner with friends.*

*Three o'clock is always too late or
too early for anything you want to do.*
— JEAN-PAUL SARTRE

One of the many beauties of knitting is that it requires little in the way of setup. Let's say you have a few minutes in the afternoon, how about a little pottery? Nope, can't do it, takes too long to set up. Maybe painting? Won't work. By the time you take out the paints and clean up the paints, your 15 minutes are gone. Knitting is perfect for quick breaks. Pick it up, do half a row, wander off again. There's no mandatory minimum amount of time. You could take three minutes a day for knitting.

*While relishing the stolen moments I can find with my knitting, I will appreciate that if I knit only three minutes a day it will take slightly less than a year to knit one sock.*

*We've begun to raise daughters more like sons . . . but few have the courage to raise our sons more like our daughters.*
— GLORIA STEINEM

For eons women have had the same complaints about men. They need to slow down, they need to remember things, they should be more patient, and they should pay attention to detail.

*Remind me again why we aren't teaching all little boys to knit?*

*Hell, there are no rules here —*
*we're trying to accomplish something.*
— THOMAS A. EDISON

I was reading a knitting book and learned, much to my horror, that you are never, ever supposed to stop in the middle of a row. This shocked me. I've been knitting for three decades; how could I have never heard this rule? Furthermore, because I haven't noticed any terrible consequence to my knitting from stopping in the middle of a row, I wonder why we're not supposed to do it. Fires? Bad karma? The plague of locusts?

*I can consider, when I encounter a knitting*
*"rule" (and feel badly about not doing it),*
*that the knitters who make up these rules*
*like to have a lot of structure.*

*I've been on a constant diet for the last two decades. I've lost a total of 789 pounds. By all accounts, I should be hanging from a charm bracelet.*

— ERMA BOMBECK

There exists, in the knitting world, a concept called "The Yarn Diet." The theory is the same as a regular diet. You purchase no new yarn and use only the yarn you have until you have "lost" the predetermined number of yarn pounds from the stash. Sadly, the result of a yarn diet is often much the same as a regular diet: a crazy woman feeling guilty as she packs on the cashmere in a yarn shop while nobody is looking.

*I will try and learn that nothing will change for me until I love my stash the way it is.*

*An ounce of prevention is*
*worth a pound of cure.*
— BENJAMIN FRANKLIN

Should you begin to suffer from wrist or hand pain while knitting, your doctor may suggest resting the hand for a day or two. The consequences of failing to rest a sore hand can result in having to sharply curtail your knitting habit for a much longer time. Many knitters have found that they can ease knitting withdrawal symptoms and temptation during this rest time by replacing knitting with one of the following activities:

- Visiting non-knitting friends (if you have any)
- Doing activities that you don't associate with knitting (if you have any)
- Drinking heavily

*I will rest when I need to, because a lifetime of these tactics has its own problems.*

# SABLE:

*a common knitting acronym that stands for Stash Acquisition Beyond Life Expectancy.*

At some point in a dedicated knitter's career, he hits this point of yarn ownership. He discovers that he has so much yarn that even if he were never to buy even one more ball or skein, and even if he were to knit full-time from now until the hour of his death, he couldn't knit it all in his lifetime. This amount of yarn is highly variable, of course, and depends on factors such as knitting speed and the age of the knitter in question.

*Achieving the state of SABLE is not, as many people who live with these knitters believe, a reason to stop buying yarn, but for the knitter it is an indication to write a will, bequeathing the stash to an appropriate heir.*

*To stay ahead, you must have your*
*next idea waiting in the wings.*
— ROSABETH MOSS KANTER

This idea is one of the foundation concepts behind keeping a substantial yarn stash. Although it may seem unbelievable to those who have not lived it, every potential project in the stash, no matter how long it has been there, was at some time supposed to be "next."

*Things change. I will be flexible.*

*I find that the harder I work,*
*the more luck I seem to have.*
— THOMAS JEFFERSON

It is a little known fact that swatches, often portrayed in knitting books as "tools," are actually magic charms. Knit a swatch and you will be protected from any number of knitting mishaps. Be arrogant enough to mock and neglect the swatch and nothing good will come of it. Necklines will fail to go over heads, sweaters will itch, and sleeves will be 9 inches too long.

*I will remember, should I think that I am above knitting a meager swatch, that knitters can be punished.*

*It is said that gifts persuade even the gods.*
— EURIPIDES

Every time somebody gives me a gift that doesn't suit me, I remind myself that it is the thought that counts. Still . . . if they were thinking, they would think yarn. I have trouble convincing people that even though I have tons of yarn, the best gift they could give me is more.

*I will remember, when someone does not give me yarn, that she was still trying to please me.*

*As a general rule the most successful man
in life is the man who has the
best information.*
— BENJAMIN DISRAELI

Sometimes I wonder about modern patterns. I wonder whether, back when knitters devised their own, they didn't learn more about knitting. Truly, to knit a sock without a pattern you need a really, really good understanding of how knitting works. It seems to me that having all the information handed to us at every turn means we don't really need to think too much.

*I reserve the right to change my mind when it turns out that knitting without a pattern teaches me about knitting way too slowly and results in a collection of knitted garments that need to be donated to the circus.*

*Opinion is that exercise of the human will which helps us to make a decision without information.*
— JOHN ERSKINE

There are two ways of providing information in a knitting pattern. The first way is written text of stitch-by-stitch instructions for each row. The second is a chart of the pattern, where the knitter follows the graph for each row, using a system of symbols. There are diehards in both camps. Some knitters will tell you that charts make them nuts; they can't remember the symbols and wish text were provided for every pattern. On the other side are the knitters who would rather lick a cactus than try to follow written instructions, citing the advantages of "seeing" the pattern reflected in the chart.

*One passionate wish all knitters share: whether words or charts, publishers should just make them bigger.*

*Cure for an obsession: get another one.*
— MASON COOLEY

It is a particular curse of my knitting career that I am destined to love shawls beyond all reason, consumed by the need to knit them, enchanted by the yarns and patterns for them, possessed by urges to buy books about them and stash many, many skeins of yarn for them . . . yet look profoundly dorky in them and know no one who would wear one.

*I can remember that, sometimes, the joy is in the doing and that shawls might make good tablecloths.*

*Solvency is entirely a matter of
temperament and not of income.*
— LOGAN PEARSALL SMITH

I hear tell of knitters who do not have a stash of yarn. They purchase yarn for a project, knit that project to completion, and then purchase the yarn for the next project. They do not have closets, bins, bags, shelves, and freezers dedicated to the storage of wool, and they have never left a yarn store with anything that they hadn't decided to buy ahead of time.

*I can try to broaden my acceptance of other styles of yarn acquirement and not assume, just because I have never met a non-stashing knitter and can't imagine being one myself, that stories about them do not belong in books next to "tooth fairy" and "Santa Claus."*

You know you
knit too much when . . .

Before you buy anything,
such as a hammock or
curtains, you seriously
wonder whether you
could knit it.

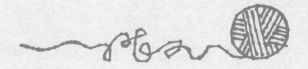

*A cat is there when you call her —*
*if she doesn't have something better to do.*
— BILL ADLER

Most cats have a thing about knitting. They are honor sworn to pester knitters and be involved in knitting as much as possible. They lie on patterns, play with balls of yarn, bat at the end of a moving needle, and given two seconds of opportunity, will spread themselves all over your knitting, intentionally shedding as much fur as possible.

*When selecting a cat to share my life and knitting with, I will consider choosing one whose fur doesn't contrast with my favorite color yarn.*

*I saw a sweater just like that at Wal-mart!*
— SOME LADY

No, you did not. Even if this sweater *looks* just like the one from Wal-mart, even if it is the same yarn, the same color, and the same size, I assure you that they are as alike as oranges and orangutans. This sweater is a handcrafted object that contains 153 hours of my life. Each stitch is here because of the sweat of my brow and the nimbleness of my fingers. THIS sweater exists only because I am a clever, determined, vital knitter, with stick-to-itiveness and an ability to follow through. Wal-mart can't touch that.

*I will open my heart and accept those who do not grasp the immense value of my knitting. They're getting a sweater from Wal-mart for Christmas, though.*

*Every path serves a purpose.*
— GENE OLIVER

I really wonder about the purpose of sewing pom-poms to the tops of hats. Given that I don't really consider them stylish or elegant and that they are a huge pain to make, I wonder what on earth prompts millions of knitters to make and sew them dutifully on millions of hats. Tradition? Style? Using up extra wool?

*As I finish the top of my daughter's hat and glare at the inevitable hole made by the gathered stitches, I will consider that pom-poms may have a deeper purpose.*

*I took a speed-reading course and
read* War and Peace *in twenty minutes.
It involves Russia.*
— WOODY ALLEN

The knitting world is full of books and patterns for "quick knits." They involve big yarn, big needles, and projects promising instant knitting gratification. I love them; they are tons and tons of fun. Finishing a hat in two hours can make you happy. Finishing a lace shawl of fine cobweb wool, however, makes you want to go into the street and accost complete strangers, forcing them to admire the shawl and be awed by your knitterly genius.

*With great effort comes great gratification. I will sometimes choose projects that will take a long time and be difficult.*

*Sanity calms, but madness is more interesting.*
— John Russell

I had a crazy aunt. This crazy aunt used to spend the whole year knitting wonderful, intricate pairs of mittens for me, my siblings, and my cousins. She made blue ones, red striped ones, ones with reindeer on them . . . there really was no end to the wonderment of mittens. Then she would box them up; half went to my cousins far away, and half to our family. There were so many in the box that during my entire childhood I never wore a mitten that came from anyone else.

It would have been a perfect thing, if only she weren't crazy. When she divided up the mittens, she would mail all the left ones to my cousins, and all the right ones to us.

*I will remember, should I get a little weird in my old age, that this strategy does not (as she had hoped) promote family unity. Nobody will drive 400 miles to swap mittens.*

*Zeus does not bring all men's plans to fulfillment.*

— HOMER

Despite the best-laid plans, the most cautious and careful knitters, the most experienced knitters, and the ones who are clever at math have all been humbled by the same crushing experience. If you knit long enough, it will happen to you, no matter what attempts you make to avoid it.

Someday, somewhere, somehow, you will run out of yarn.

*I will remember, when my day comes, that there is one magic word that can help: STRIPES.*

*Really we create nothing.*
*We merely plagiarize nature.*
— JEAN BAITAILLON

Sunlight dapples through green maple leaves at the park and gives me the perfect idea for a Fair Isle colorway. I'll use the greens in dark and light shades, the brown of the bark in the shade, and the gold of the branches in sunshine. I feel so artistic, like I'm connected to the great masters who painted scenes much like this. They mixed paints on their palettes, I'll pull yarn from the stash and shops, but we are all artists striving to re-create the natural world with our talents.

Two weeks later, as I'm desperately scrounging through the bins at the seventeenth yarn shop I've visited, I'm realizing that the exact lime green of sunlight striking the top leaves does not exist in the yarn world. I wonder whether I'm the first knitter to think that Michelangelo and van Gogh had it easy. They could mix the color they needed.

*I will remember that every medium has its limits. Maybe I can't get the exact color I need, but Michelangelo would have had a hard time carving something that felt like angora.*

*It is a mistake to try to look too far ahead.*
*The chain of destiny can only be grasped*
*one link at a time.*
— SIR WINSTON CHURCHILL

Especially for beginning knitters, a complex pattern can be daunting. You look at a pattern and are over-whelmed by the 46 rows in a lace pattern, or think that you are going to cry in public at some point during the short-row cap sleeve, or that you will lose hours of sleep gnashing your teeth and end up with only a tattered pile of knitted crap.

*Before I cast aside my destiny (and a pattern for a spectacular lace coverlet), I will consider that all knitting, no matter how complex, how huge, or how intimidating, was knit one row at a time.*

You know you
knit too much when . . .

You will check out a book
from the library just because
you heard that one of the
characters knits.

*The only way to get rid of a temptation*
*is to yield to it.*
— OSCAR WILDE

With my wool as my witness I will swear that yarn emits resolve-impairing rays. There is no other possible explanation for why a perfectly normal woman like me can go into a yarn shop determined to buy only a set of double-pointed needles and leave with 18 skeins of blue wool, a shawl kit, two books, and a quirky self-patterning sock yarn.

*I will support all attempts by science to explain this effect.*

*The statistics on sanity are that*
*one out of every four Americans*
*is suffering from some form of*
*mental illness. Think of your three*
*best friends. If they're okay, then it's you.*
— RITA MAE BROWN

One of the most interesting things about knitting is that it causes a delayed sense of clarity. A knitter can stand in a yarn shop and plan, purchase wool for, and explain to friends her plan to knit a cover for a king-size bed out of fingering-weight yarn using 3mm needles and not ever once, even for a moment, consider that insane until after she has started the project.

*I will remember, should my friends in the yarn shop giggle as I purchase my wool, to run a quick "sanity check" on my idea.*

*The art of being wise is the art of*
*knowing what to overlook.*
— WILLIAM JAMES

I am done with the back of my friend's sweater. My friend is 6'4" and . . . er, robust . . . and it is only through sheer will that I have knit the front and endless sleeves. It may have been a tactical error to make those allover cables in black; in fact, trying to see the cables has been at times staggeringly difficult, and if I ever am completely blind, I'm going to know which sweater to blame. Suddenly, I see it. At the bottom of the sweater there is one miscrossed cable. I feel nauseous and the world swirls around me in darkening circles as I think about reknitting the entire back. I know I'll never be able to live with the mistake.

*I will remember, should I ever find myself in a similar situation, that I don't have to live with the mistake at all. I can sew the thing up and give it away.*

*Experience is something you don't get*
*until just after you need it.*
— STEVEN WRIGHT

When I was six, I spent an afternoon in my grandmother's garden with my needles, yarn, and what I thought was a darned good idea. It occurred to me that I could save myself all kinds of time while knitting if I didn't have to turn my work at the end of each row. When I had it completely figured, I traipsed up to the house, found my Nana, and showed her my incredible invention — backward knitting. My very proper Nana said this was simply "not how it was done." Chastised, I returned to conventional frontward knitting, and it wasn't until last night when I was working on a five-stitch strap that I remembered. I could have been really good at that by now.

*I will not let anyone tell me what a good knitting idea is.*

*Find something you're passionate about and
keep tremendously interested in it.*
— Julia Child

I know a knitter whose husband is starting to worry a little because his wife appears to have become completely obsessed with a movie star. At least, that's what he thinks, because she has rented the same movie about 15 times just so she can stare intently at the male lead. I know better; she has confessed that she's actually obsessed with the sweater the guy's wearing and has been trying to puzzle out the pattern for months. She hasn't told her husband because she's worried that he will think she's completely out of her mind.

*Consider that your husband might actually be relieved that you are oddly drawn to a sweater, rather than believing that his wife has developed a completely unhealthy attraction to a 19-year-old.*

*Love is always bestowed as a gift —*
*freely, willingly and without expectation.*
*We don't love to be loved; we love to love.*
— LEO BUSCAGLIA

In every knitter's stash there are a few skeins of yarn that were purchased with absolutely no purpose in mind. The knitter knows, though she may never admit it, that this yarn isn't looking for its destiny either. It will never, ever be knit. Its sole purpose in the knitter's life is to be beautiful and to be loved.

*This yarn and its role are perfectly normal, though a knitter should understand that other knitters will mock her, much as we sometimes mock the older man who marries a young lovely, for having acquired "trophy yarn."*

*A home without books is a body without soul.*
— Cicero

This quote applies as well to knitters as it does to scholars, poets, and writers. The knitter's urge to procure and hoard a lifetime supply of yarn is only one side of the obsession with knitting. The other is a profound and deep need to buy an incredible number of books, patterns, magazines, and newsletters that talk about yarn, knitting, and the ways of needles.

*Although the mountains of written material most knitters have in their homes would seem unnatural and odd, it is only the normal extension of a deep interest in knitting and the human desire to better oneself in one's chosen art.*

*That, and the pictures are pretty.*

*Reality is the leading cause of stress*
*for those in touch with it.*
— JACK WAGNER

M ost of the stress associated with learning to knit is not caused by knitting but by an inability to fix errors. Pity the poor knitter who can't fix a mistake; every time she makes one, she has to start her project over. Wise knitting mentors teach students at the first sitting to pick up a dropped stitch so that they are not living in paralyzed fear of a little woolen loop that has broken free of the needle.

*Consider telling those you teach that no matter how it feels to the new knitter, a dropped stitch has never actually caused stroke, heart failure, or a world war.*

You know you
knit too much when ...

You are so excited about the
yarn you just bought that
you buy new size 5 knitting
needles (even though you
have nine pairs at home)
so that you can start your
project on the bus ride home
from the yarn shop.

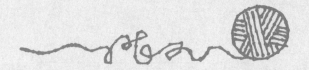

*Learning without thought is labor lost;*
*thought without learning is perilous.*

— CONFUCIUS

Learning to do cables without a cable needle is a liberating feeling. Once you have mastered the technique, it is faster, easier, and more efficient.

*Should I feel reluctant to learn this technique, I will remind myself of how inevitable it is that I will lose my cable needle anyway.*

*A fool and his money are soon partying.*
— STEVEN WRIGHT

I don't know what it says about me that if I get a little money, and I want to go nuts and have a really good time . . . enjoy a real blowout celebration, cut loose, go wild, and lose all my inhibitions . . . that I will go to the biggest, wildest, fanciest yarn shop in town.

*I will celebrate the happy events of my life in a way that makes sense to me, and besides, yarn has more staying power and less of a hangover than tequila does.*

*Sculpture is the art of the intelligence.*
— PABLO PICASSO

It is an incredibly charming and clever trick that knitting is one long piece of string. It is not like building blocks or bricks, made up of individual pieces, but more like sculpting in clay, where the material is shaped by your intentions and creativity.

*I will remember that the downside to this fancy trick is that a two-year-old left alone with knitting for three minutes can undo the better part of a shawl, just by pulling on that one string.*

*Let each man exercise the art he knows.*
— ARISTOPHANES

Imagine a knitter. This knitter, having taken a trip to the beach, has become obsessed with knitting a scarf in the exact shade of the ocean. She is not trying to capture the entire ocean in wool, but only the part near the edge of the bay, right where the water gets deep. Since she has returned from the beach, she has scoured stashes, yarn shops, and Internet sources, searching fruitlessly for yarn that is the exact, perfect, marine blue. This behavior is normal, but this knitter is not. Most knitters, defeated by yarn unavailability, would spend the rest of their lives happy, but always looking for that yarn. This knitter . . . she has bought some dye.

*Occasionally, the universe conspires to keep something from you so you can learn new things. Look for those chances to expand your chosen art form.*

*Money talks — but credit has an echo.*
— BOB THAVES

Most knitters, if they were to be completely honest with you, would have to confess that the place their credit card gets the most use is in a yarn shop. When I was done being a student, I had two kinds of debt: student loans and yarn loans.

*Think carefully before buying yarn on credit. You should at least be able to pay for it sometime before it is knit up. (For most of us, this is not a powerful deterrent.)*

*Remorse is the echo of a lost virtue.*
— EDWARD ROBERT BULWER-LYTTON

I have, once or twice (which is a pretty good track record, when you think of it), felt remorse over time "wasted" knitting or a particularly extravagant yarn buy. I usually manage to rationalize myself into feeling good about it again, and I have found a very efficient remorse eraser. I'll share it now, in case you are ever tempted by remorse:

*I am not wasting time knitting or wasting money buying yarn. I am creating useful and beautiful objects that will outlast me and my days. I am creating a legacy to outlive me.*

*All you need is love.*
— JOHN LENNON

Well, that's a nice thought, but you can't knit love, baby.

*Even as I strive to reduce the complexity of my life to encompass only most of the basic elements of human happiness, I will remember that even though John Lennon said, "All you need is love," I'm not giving up my yarn. After all, he never gave up his guitar.*

*The essence of education is the*
*education of the body.*
— BENJAMIN DISRAELI

I was teaching a children's knitting class, and one poor little guy absolutely could not get it. This was profoundly disappointing to him, because he had announced when arriving that he was already a pretty good knitter. Over and over he tried, over and over he dropped stitches. Finally, I put my hands over his and together we made a stitch, then another and another, and pretty soon he was flying solo.

When his mother arrived, he proudly showed her his two rows of perfectly solid knitting. "I thought you already knew how to knit," his mother said. "I did," he replied. "But it took a while for my hands to catch on."

*I will remember, the next time I am frustrated with my knitting, that the problem might not be me . . . but my hands.*

*If at first you don't succeed,*
*failure may be your style.*
— QUENTIN CRISP

If it turns out that you are the kind of knitter who makes mistakes often (not that I can relate), then you are very lucky. You are going to learn lots of stuff about knitting that those simple, perfect knitters will never have the chance to learn. For example, just the other day I heard about a knitter (not me, of course) who invented a new way to increase when she accidentally knit into both parts of a split stitch.

*I will embrace my imperfect nature and take what good comes of it, resisting the urge to mock flawless knitters who don't invent anything.*

You know you
knit too much when . . .

You are at the video store
renting a movie and reject
a film with subtitles because
the project you are knitting
has a chart.

Everybody knows that you
can't read subtitles if you
are already reading a chart.

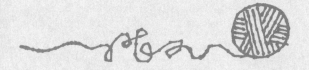

*100% pure wool, 50g,*
*120 yards/110 meters*

— YARN LABEL

I have checked every single ball band on every single ball and skein of yarn I have ever bought and none of them, not even one, has ever listed a warning about the addictive qualities of the product contained within.

I know that this is a clear omission, because it's not possible that yarn is not addictive, given what happens to most people who buy some.

*Just because the world hasn't figured out what I know to be true does not mean that I am wrong. For years people said that cigarettes weren't addictive. I will wait for science to catch up with me.*

*Grown-ups never understand anything for themselves, and it is tiresome for children to be always and forever explaining things to them.*
— ANTOINE DE SAINT-EXUPERY

My young daughter was enjoying a play date with a child she knew from school, and the two youngsters were playing hide-and-seek when the little girl's mother arrived to take her home. The girls where hiding, so the mother made a game of hunting for them. She looked under the table, behind the chesterfield, then spied a closet and flung it open. Imagine her shock when inside were not only two little girls but also a literal wall of yarn.

"Wow," she said. "What's this?"

"It's one of our yarn closets," my daughter told her, looking at her like she had just asked the purpose of our stove.

"A yarn closet?" the mother replied, clearly astonished.

"Yeah," said my daughter, slowly and carefully, like she was speaking to someone very stupid, "you know . . . where you keep your yarn?"

*Sometimes, children see things so clearly.*

*A woman will buy anything she thinks*
*the store is losing money on.*
— KIN HUBBARD

Insert "knitter" for "woman" in the quotation above and you have the beginnings of an explanation for what seems like 70 pounds of super-cheap, butt-ugly, army green kitchen cotton that I have sitting in the yarn stash.

*I will persist in believing that I was stunned into submission by the deeply discounted price on this yarn, because the alternative is to accept that I really have no taste.*

*Not a shred of evidence exists in favor*
*of the idea that life is serious.*
— BRENDAN GILL

I try to keep this quotation in mind whenever it seems to me that I might have to cry because my knitting isn't working out. Making mistakes in knitting isn't a serious problem. It's just knitting; it's supposed to be a fun hobby. It isn't supposed to be a process that stresses you out and causes upset, anger, or the urge to put a needle into your thigh.

I will reserve that honor for accidentally throwing a hand knit in the washing machine.

*Nobody has ever been killed by his or her knitting.*

*I value my garden more for being full of blackbirds than of cherries, and very frankly give them fruit for their songs.*

— JOSEPH ADDISON

As I am a woman of little patience, I occasionally set fleece and yarn in my backyard to dry. The fresh air dries it very quickly, and it makes me very happy to see the pretty colors of the wool drying next to the flowers and trees. I feel like I'm at one with nature. The birds sing, the garden blooms, and my wool dries in the pretty sunshine.

*I will try to retain this feeling, even as I notice that the thieving little birds are ripping off my yarn for nest materials.*

You know you
knit too much when . . .

Your kids complain that
you are paying too much
attention to your knitting,
so you switch to a garter
stitch project.

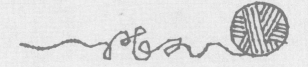

*Respect yourself and others will respect you.*
— Confucius

Perhaps because knitting is mostly done by women, or perhaps because it is considered by some to be one of the "domestic arts," such as sweeping or doing the dishes, there is a tendency, even among those of us who do it, to consider it simple, frivolous, or unworthy.

*I will remember, the next time someone asks me about my hobby, to refrain from calling it "just knitting."*

*If you rest, you rust.*

— HELEN HAYES

My Auntie Helen is very old. She is so old, in fact, that everyone in the family has lost track of how old exactly she might be, though we all agree that she is well past ninety. She has always knit mittens for us, and even now, though her hands get sore and her eyesight is failing her, she continues to knit, only from memory instead of from a pattern. If you ask her what the secret to her vibrant and productive old age is, she'll tell you that you just need to keep moving.

*As I grow older, I can hope that I will continue to knit . . . even if I can't read a pattern. It will help me keep moving.*

*Youth is a wonderful thing.*
*What a crime to waste it on children.*
— GEORGE BERNARD SHAW

I have taught all my children and plenty of other people's children how to knit. Most kids are capable of it at about the age of five, and it is a real treat to watch a youngster discover the joys of knitting and hold up a misshapen little scarf, thrilled to be able to say "I made it myself."

*Always remember, should you decide to pass on your knitting knowledge to the next generation, that kids have a natural aptitude for handiwork, a knack for learning, and given half a chance, are absolutely driven to poke each other with pointy sticks.*

*I just need enough to tide me over
until I need more.*

— BILL HOEST

3 signs you have a serious yarn habit:

1. You have invested money in a yarn storage solution that involves more than one room of your house.
2. You can feel your heart stall for a second when you see a moth.
3. When you moved to another city, the lady who owns the yarn shop in your old neighborhood had her car repossessed.

*For every problem there is a solution*
*which is simple, clean and wrong.*
— HENRY LOUIS MENCKEN

Having discovered that I made a critical error knitting the cap sleeves of a sweater, I sat down and had a little think about it. The answer came to me quickly. (Perhaps too quickly.) Because the problem was that the shoulder parts of the sleeves were now too big, I realized that I could simply add more room to the shoulder area of the front and back. It was beautiful in its simplicity, and I didn't have to reknit the sleeves.

*I am working toward accepting that I apparently missed my calling. I should be knitting football uniforms. The thing is perfect for a linebacker.*

*Nothing deters a good man from
doing what is honorable.*

— SENECA

Being a knitting mother leads to certain challenges. It is difficult to find the time to knit, it is hard to keep toddlers from pulling the needles from your knitting, and it is even harder to keep a new baby from spitting up on the new blanket you made. The hardest thing, however, the most certain challenge for a knitting mother, is trying to make your kids be good for two hours in a yarn shop.

*I will remember that desperate times call for desperate measures, and that bribing a kid with money or candy can be honorable if you do it right.*

*If we see you smoking*
*we will assume you are on fire*
*and take appropriate action.*
— DOUGLAS ADAMS

People knit for their own reasons, but some of the most intense knitters I know are the ones who used it to help them quit smoking. It's a perfect plan, really; knitting keeps your hands busy, and it is relaxing and repetitive enough to hold off most of the urges to smoke. You get to spend your cigarette money on yarn, a powerful motivator, and two weeks after you quit you have four sweaters, three hats, and several really big afghans.

*Knitting can be a useful tool for self-improvement.*

*I adore simple pleasures.*
*They are the last refuge of the complex.*
— OSCAR WILDE

Lots of knitters knit washcloths, and lots of other knitters make fun of them for it. Simple or fancy, these humble little squares of cotton appear by the millions in some knitters' homes, along with patterns for them by the hundreds. Knitters who love them say they are the softest cloths you can get, they can be made to match the bathroom perfectly, and they are a gentle exfoliator . . . making you a younger-looking knitter. These knitters claim they love trying out different stitches on something small, and that they get a kick out of a cheap, easy project.

*Before I mock the simple art of washcloth knitting, I will consider how good it would feel to finish four projects in a day.*

You know you
knit too much when ...

You hear that a friend is
going though a difficult
time, and even though this
friend doesn't knit, you
consider dropping yarn off
at her house to make her
feel better.

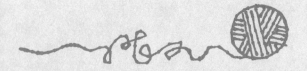

*The art of war is simple enough. Find out where your enemy is. Get at him as soon as you can. Strike him as hard as you can, and keep moving.*

— ULYSSES S. GRANT

The one time I found a moth in my stash, some thought that I over-reacted. I cleaned, vacuumed, froze, baked, or microwaved every skein of yarn that I had; threw away anything I could possibly live without. Then I put all the yarn that had been anywhere near the moth into baggies and placed them in quarantine. My best and most precious yarn was placed in a deep freezer, dedicated solely to wool storage. The rest of the yarn entered a strict sur-veillance program, which has continued for years. Even though I have never seen another moth, I have not lessened my state of constant vigilance.

*There is no way to overreact to a moth.*

*Nothing is as simple as we hope it will be.*
— Jim Horning

I was teaching a knitting class and had started the group with the most basic scarf project in the world. The pattern is so simple that I will give it to you here. Browse the yarn shop until you find a worsted-weight yarn you adore. On 5mm needles, cast on 40 stitches, then knit every stitch of every row until your yarn is almost gone or you think the scarf is long enough. Cast off.

The class sat diligently, knitting every stitch of every row until the hour was up, then packed up their things and left.

An hour later I got a phone call from one of the scarf knitters in the class. "I'm so glad you are still there," she said. "I forgot my pattern. Can you fax it to me? I want to keep working on my scarf."

*Everyone learns at her own pace. I can resist the urge to tease the stragglers.*

> *The road of excess leads to*
> *the palace of wisdom.*
> —WILLIAM BLAKE

**5** reasons to hoard yarn:

1. If you get enough of it, yarn can act as house insulation.
2. Yarns get discontinued. Think about that, then buy accordingly.
3. Nobody is ever going to understand how seriously you take knitting if you don't have lots of yarn as proof.
4. Yarn has absolutely no expiration date.
5. Hairless cats appeared in Toronto in 1963. What if that happens to sheep? What if it spreads? What if all that is left in the world is what you have?

*I will not try to limit my yarn supply any more than an artist tries to limit his paints.*

*I became insane, with long intervals of horrible sanity!*
— EDGAR ALLAN POE

Dear Designer whose name I shall not mention to be polite,

If you think that I need to start seeing a therapist you could have just told me. There was no need to conduct this charade. You knew I would buy this pattern, you knew that the yarn would be discontinued, you knew that there would be no way that I would ever be able to achieve gauge with any other yarn in the world no matter how many I tried, and you knew that this would turn me into a delusional raving maniac. I give up. I am going to make a king-size afghan out of the hundreds of swatches I have knit during the time I spent working on it and forget that I ever saw this sweater.

Let's never speak of this again.

*Difficult patterns are not necessarily a personal issue. I will not mail this letter.*

*As I work among my flowers, I find myself talking to them, reasoning and remonstrating with them, and adoring them as if they were human beings. Much laughter I provoke among my friends by so doing, but that is of no consequence. We are on such good terms, my flowers and I.*

— CELIA THAXTER

Some knitters say that they buy yarn with no project in mind and wait patiently for the yarn to "speak" to them. This reminds me of Michelangelo, who believed that every block of stone he carved had the statue waiting inside and that all he did was reveal it. I think I've had yarn speak to me during the knitting process, and I've definitely spoken to it. Perhaps I'm doing it wrong, or maybe my yarn and I aren't on such good terms, but it really seems to me that all I say is "please" and all it ever says is "no."

> *Friendship is a strong and*
> *habitual inclination in two persons*
> *to promote the good and*
> *happiness of one another.*
> — EUSTACE BUDGELL

I have a friend named Laurie. She lives very far away from me, and I have to content myself with e-mails and letters and the occasional surprise package. Besides being a clever and thoughtful woman, Laurie is a genius. She spins and knits and dyes the most beautiful things, and there is not a day that I don't think of her and wish that I lived closer to her, just so that I could have the pleasure of her company and the comfortable reassurance that there is someone else out there who is definitely as insane about knitting as I am. Some time ago, Laurie dyed some wool, spun it into sock yarn, and mailed it to me. I knit it up into the most beautiful and comfortable socks I have ever owned. The heels are a little bit wonky (I screwed them up a little), but they remain the best things I can put on my feet. They feel like a joint effort, Laurie's spinning and my knitting, and whenever the world gets a little bit tough I put them on. They are tangible evidence that I am never alone and friendless.

*I will never diminish the magical powers of knitting, where friendship can be mailed in 200 yards of homespun.*

*Better three hours too soon*
*than a minute too late.*
— WILLIAM SHAKESPEARE

My husband, an otherwise wonderful human being, has a fairly loose relationship with time. He is seldom punctual, and even less often aware that he is late. If I added up all the time that I spend waiting for him, 15 minutes here, 10 minutes there . . . I would probably have to divorce him instantly in a fit of outrage. Instead, because I have the miracle of knitting to save my marriage, I sit happily each time, patiently knitting until he arrives.

*I will consider that my husband might work harder to be on time if I would stop rewarding him with the socks that I knit while waiting.*

*Always remember you're unique,*
*just like everyone else.*
— ALISON BOULTER

One time when I was at a party the conversation turned to knitting and how much fun it is and how everybody should do it. (I may have been the only one talking right then.) A woman stood right across from me, looked me in the eye, and told me that she had tried knitting and that it wasn't fun, it was sort of dumb and boring. She hadn't liked it at all.

I stared at her like she had a third eye. I've always thought that if somebody didn't care for knitting it was because they hadn't tried it. To have done it and not be captivated by the wonder of it was inconceivable.

*I will try to accept that knitting is not for everyone, but really know that if she didn't like knitting . . . she wasn't doing it right.*

*I don't believe in stereotypes,*
*I prefer to hate people on*
*a more personal basis.*

— Anonymous

There are those who believe that knitting is still the province of elderly women with nothing better to do. They think that it is a rocking chair activity that a young lady might participate in only if she is expecting a baby or is a little more boring, lonely, or friendless than we had all hoped for. Simple proof that knitting has broken free of the bonds of this stereotype can be had by anyone with access to the Internet. A two-minute search will reveal patterns for willie warmers, thongs, and lingerie, definitely intended for knitters who leave their houses and have active social lives.

*By acknowledging the diversity of knitters,*
*I can celebrate it without needing to knit*
*a really itchy thong.*

*I didn't do very well in math — I could never seem to persuade the teacher that I hadn't meant my answers literally.*

— CALVIN TRILLIN

Myriad ways have been devised to help knitters keep track of how many rows they have knit or where they are in a pattern. Some knitters use a row counter; others use a clicker. Many make marks on a piece of paper, and some cross out instructions on the pattern as they complete them. Being somewhat numerically challenged, the best idea I ever heard was to use M&Ms. If you have 32 rows to knit, then you make a pile of 32 candies beside you. At the end of each row, you eat one. When they are gone, you are done. Brilliant in its simplicity, isn't it?

*Remember that this technique can result in screwy socks and really short sweaters if you have children and leave your knitting unattended.*

You know you
knit too much when . . .

You take knitting to a
wedding, in case there's a
little time before the bride
comes down the aisle.

Double points if you are
the bride.

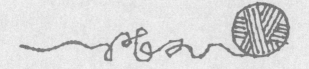

*The nice thing about being a celebrity
is that when you bore people,
they think it's their fault.*
— HENRY KISSINGER

Sally Fields, Daryl Hannah, Julianne Moore, Brooke Shields, Bridget Fonda, Tyra Banks, Debra Messing, Caroline Rhea, Laurence Fishburne, Justine Bateman, Russell Crowe, Uma Thurman, Madonna, Cameron Diaz, Madeleine Albright, Kate Moss, Eartha Kitt, Sandra Bullock, Hilary Swank, Karen Allen, Sarah Jessica Parker, Joanne Woodward, Elizabeth Taylor, Stu Bloomberg, Goldie Hawn, and Jennifer Aniston all knit and buy yarn.

*I do not need the endorsement of celebrities to make me think knitting is cool. I think it's pretty neat that they all want to be like me.*

*There's a fine line between genius and*
*insanity. I have erased this line.*
— OSCAR LEVANT

It takes a special kind of knitter to truly understand knitting. These knitters can be identified by their advanced knitting skills, the evolved and cunning nature of their work, and a deep understanding of the knitter's art. Other subtle hints include round-the-clock stitching, yarn in every room of the house, and an unnatural interest in the reverse side of store-bought sweaters.

*I am not obsessed. I am gaining experience.*

*If you knew what I know about the power
of giving, you would not let a single meal
pass without sharing it in some way.*

— BUDDHA

I taught all my children to knit, and
mostly I am glad that I did. It's a
double-edged sword, though. On the
one hand, I now live with delightful
daughters who enjoy one of the same
things that I do, and it's not often that
you get to have that kind of common
ground with a teenager. On the other
hand, they think we should all share
my yarn.

*I will try to be generous about giving my
children my wool, even though I have already
given them a place to live, food to eat, and
the best years of my life.*

*It is very difficult to live among people you love and hold back from offering them advice.*
— ANNE TYLER

In the early spring I knit my daughter a beautiful pair of green and yellow socks. They reminded me of sunshine on the new leaves in the garden. I imagined my willowy young daughter in the socks and it made me happy. Part of the joy of knitting is imagining the items in use, and while I was knitting them I loved the idea that she would look so beautiful and elegant, especially when she wore them with her new spring coat.

*I will remember that they belong to her once given, and that I have no right to rip the socks right off her ungrateful little feet when she puts them on with hot-pink tights and combat boots.*

*Creativity is allowing yourself to make
mistakes. Art is knowing which ones to keep.*
— SCOTT ADAMS

Mistakes in knitting are inevitable. Don't panic; you have options. Some patient knitters unknit their work one stitch at a time until they reach the mistake, unknit that, and have a do-over. This is time-consuming, but it works very well. Other experienced knitters choose to drop the stitches in the offending section, unravel them until they reach the error, then carefully retrieve the stitches and knit them back up correctly. A crochet hook can help. Bold knitters take the work off the needles completely, rip the work back, replace the needle, and go onward. The cleverest knitters ask themselves, "Is there any way I could repeat this error on the other side to make this a design feature?"

*I will allow myself to consider "nontraditional" solutions to a knitting error.*

*Being defeated is often a temporary condition.*
*Giving up is what makes it permanent.*
— MARILYN VOS SAVANT

Entrelac is a technique in knitting whereby a knitter creates a fascinating and beautiful multidirectional fabric by knitting little squares in opposite directions. Some knitters enjoy this to no end and advocate learning to knit backward to simplify the knitting of the millions of little squares. These knitters are patient and talented. In my experience, however, if you enjoy knitting entrelac, you may also want to try pulling all your nose hair out with tweezers.

*I will feel free to dump a knitting technique that threatens my sanity and happiness.*

*An idea can turn to dust or magic,*
*depending on the talent that rubs against it.*
— WILLIAM BERNBACH

For Christmas one year I made my sister-in-law Kate a "magic scarf." The general idea is that you knit a scarf about one-third the length you would like it to be, then drop every other stitch as you cast off. This done, you pull both ends of the scarf, the dropped stitches run freely to the cast-on edge, and poof!, the scarf lengthens by about two-thirds. I imagined that working this magic would be sort of fun for Kate, so I left the scarf unpulled, tucked the instructions into the box, and sent it off. A year later I found out that Kate had missed the instruction sheet but had appreciated the stumpy little scarf and worn it dutifully for a year, even though it practically strangled her.

*We can remember to look for the subtle signs that people appreciate our knitting.*

*Many men have been capable of doing
a wise thing, more a cunning thing,
but very few a generous thing.*
— ALEXANDER POPE

My sister-in-law Kelly is a knitter and a generous person. Like many knitters, she gives away most of what all that she knits. Kelly had her eye on these beautiful one-of-a-kind hanks of yarn, imagining (finally) the most beautiful shawl for herself, and when the right color came along, she snapped it up. Weeks were spent on the shawl, and she ultimately finished her masterpiece while traveling to a friend's home. When she arrived, she found a birthday party in full swing. Kelly was horrified for a minute that she had no gift; then it all became terribly clear. She brokenheartedly wrapped up her dream shawl and handed it over.

*I will strive to accept that my knitting may have a destiny separate from my own.*

*Hardy folks don't run from change;*
*they exult in its challenges.*

— Anonymous

Knitters have been devastated that, in some places, security restrictions have resulted in knitting needles being banned from planes. A knitter I know was taking a very long flight and simply couldn't imagine not knitting. She and her husband put their heads together and came up with paper knitting needles. Tightly coil thin strips of paper, then pull out the center to make a long, pointed taper. Coat it with ordinary white glue to make it a little tougher, and you have a knitting needle that won't set off X-ray machines or be considered dangerous like wood, metal, or plastic. She happily knit all the way to Australia.

*I will try to be understanding about the rules and resist the urge to explain that I'm a bigger risk without my needles than with them.*

*Imagine if every Thursday your shoes
exploded if you tied them the usual way. This
happens to us all the time with computers,
and nobody thinks of complaining.*
— JEFF RASKIN

Knitting has a big home on the Internet and within computers. Blogs (web logs) journal knitters' work, patterns, and innovations, yarn shops have online shopping to let you buy yarn from an independent spinner across the world, and online groups connect knitters from around the world. You can buy software that designs sweaters, tracks your yarn purchases, or prints knitter's graph paper or colorways for Fair Isle. At first this marriage between knitting and computers struck me as odd. Knitting seems like the opposite of computers, and I couldn't image that the two were compatible. That didn't last long. When I found out I could join a virtual knitting circle and ask 7,000 knitters worldwide what they thought I was doing wrong with buttonholes, I was hooked.

*I will remember, should I choose to explore the virtual knitting world, that you can knit while using the computer if you put the keyboard on the floor and scroll with your toes.*

# SSS:

*an abbreviation referring to the crippling and common knitter's affliction known as Second Sock Syndrome.*

SSS afflicts millions of knitters around the world, with conservative estimates claiming that 95 percent of knitters have suffered at some point in their sock-knitting careers, while a full 99 percent of knitters live in fear.

Knitters with SSS happily knit the first sock of a pair, enjoying the yarn, the pattern, and the process. When that sock is finished, they then find themselves completely and inexplicably unable to knit the second sock. At this point, knitters with SSS feel boredom, monotony, and the overwhelming urge to begin a new and unrelated pair of socks. Sadly, SSS is a repeating disease, and when the knitter casts on a new pair of socks, the cycle begins again.

Although we used to believe that SSS was contagious and spread from knitter to knitter, we now understand that it is spread by sock yarn itself. SSS is not fatal, but it can lead to an embarrassing number of single hand-knit socks and lone balls of yarn.

*Should I begin to exhibit symptoms, I will treat SSS by immediately casting on the second sock, and avoid starting a pair of mittens at all costs.*

*A deadline is negative inspiration.*
*Still, it's better than no inspiration at all.*
— RITA MAE BROWN

My husband is a big guy. One year, as the holidays approached, I was overcome by the urge to display my love for him in wool. I rummaged through the stash and came up with enough wool to knit him a beautiful long-sleeved Aran sweater. I did the math for his 48-inch chest and surprisingly long arms, came up with a pattern, and began the immense task of knitting him a roomy sweater. I slogged through the front, then began the back, realizing with each stitch that I was in over my head. As much as I love him, as desperate as I was to make him something nice, I felt my strength falter as I knit each row of the enormous back, wishing all the while that I was married to somebody smaller, or that the holiday was further away. When I was finally finished, I poured myself a glass of wine and tried to face casting on the sleeves for what now seemed like his freakishly long arms. Suddenly the answer came to me. I didn't need a smaller husband; I needed to make a vest.

*An open mind is a powerful thing. I will leave room in my plans for inspiration.*

*The only Zen you find on tops of mountains
is the Zen you bring there.*
— ROBERT M. PIRSIG

I had chosen to knit a plain navy cardigan. It was boring me to tears but left me lots of time to think. As I knit it, I realized what purpose it was here to fulfill. It was a Zen sweater, with no distracting color, style, or stitch pattern. Just miles and miles of pure, unadulterated, mind-numbing stockinette stitch, without any of the distracting design elements to stand between me and its sweater essence.

I gave in to it and its lesson for me, and became one with the sweater. I was given the opportunity to reflect on my act of knitting and enter a simple meditative state, where I was capable of deep inner realization and reflection. In this trancelike state, you can reach deep introspective places, ask complex questions of your inner self, find answers that lead to greater harmony with your spirit, and have the opportunity to become more fully centered as a human being.

*I will work toward becoming a better person so that my deep questions aren't just, "Will this boring sweater never end?" or, "What am I . . . a masochist?"*

*To love deeply in one direction
makes us more loving in all others.*
— ANNE-SOPHIE SWETCHINE

I love to knit. It is my reward for good behavior, my friend when I am lonely or impatient, and a constant source of entertainment when I am bored. I appreciate that I am getting to be productive and feel happy that I am being useful and clever, using two pointy sticks to turn common yarn into things that will long outlast me. Each stitch makes something that was not there before, and this simple act of creation fills me up.

*I will not make apologies for thoroughly enjoying the pleasant act of knitting. You can call me crazy or obsessive, but I still say that this makes more sense than golf.*

*This is my simple religion. There is no need for temples; no need for complicated philosophy. Our own brain, our own heart is our temple; the philosophy is kindness.*
— DALAI LAMA

There are knitters who find that the practice of knitting, done mindfully and meditatively, can be a spiritual one. Some of these knitters make prayer shawls for others who need their thoughts, love, and concern during a difficult time. Each shawl is knit as religious expression, and each stitch is infused with love, gentleness, and good wishes for those who need it most. The lucky recipients of this act of kindness say that they can feel the support and love of the knitter when they wrap the shawl around their shoulders.

*I respect the intent of these shawls and the fine purpose with which they are knit. I will make one as soon as I learn not to curse when I drop a stitch, because I worry about what I'd infuse it with.*

*Trust your instinct to the end,*
*though you can render no reason.*
— RALPH WALDO EMERSON

I wonder about my fascination with hunting for knitting magazines. I stalk them in shops, checking every store until I have collected all of a season's issues, practically laughing out loud when I score one at the grocery store. I make opportunities to walk past big bookstores so that I can casually nip inside and scour the shelves for them. I buy them without looking inside to see whether there is anything good, get jealous if I find out some other knitter bagged one before I did, and have occasionally purchased the same issue twice because I got a little excited.

*I accept this as normal behavior, and accept that my unwillingness to get a subscription is a throwback to primitive humans' hunter-gatherer instincts.*

You know you
knit too much when . . .

You show up at your favorite
yarn shop's huge annual sale
and, before you can go in
and shop with the other
knitters, the owner takes
you aside to remind you that
she doesn't want a repeat of
what happened last year.

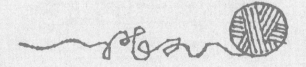

*One of the most obvious facts about grownups
to a child is that they have forgotten what
it is like to be a child.*

— RANDALL JARRELL

My friend Ken was knitting on a bus during his daily commute. He was working on a sock and using five very fine metal double-pointed needles. Ken's a quick knitter, and the little boy in the seat in front of him was turned around to watch, very interested in the flashing needles.

"What are you doing?" the little boy asked.

"Knitting a sock," replied Ken, smiling warmly at the boy. The little lad watched intently for a few more minutes before a mischievous grin crept across his face.

"It looks dangerous," he said.

*People knit for their own reasons. I will
remember this little boy and consider giving
kids his age plastic needles with which to
learn.*

You know you
knit too much when . . .

Without your knitting,
you feel lonely.

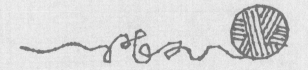

*Mi taku oyasin. [We are all related.]*
— LAKOTA SAYING

You may be an only child. Perhaps you are the only man in a knitting guild or, like me, quite short and never in control of your laundry.

It doesn't matter, for you are a knitter, and to belong completely, no matter how different you may appear to be. . . .

*. . . all you need to do is find more knitters.*

# Acknowledgments

Without the help of these people, there would be no book. My flock is to be thanked.

Storey Publishing, for coming up with the idea, thinking that I could do it, and making the birth as painless as possible.

Siobhan Dunn and Deborah Balmuth, my editors, who were patient and clever.

Linda Roghaar, my really good agent, who put up with countless neurotic, paranoid, panicked phone calls and who totally gets the whole knitting thing.

Bonnie McPhee, my mother, who taught me that the written word is a force to be reckoned with, phoned me with quotations all the time, and never acted like writing wasn't a real job.

Kelly Dunphy, for thinking of the perfect thing to do when I was stuck (twice).

Ken Allen, my dear friend, who lent me a laptop so I could write in the park, gave me wool for my birthday, and never thought that liking knitting this much was dorky.

Lene Andersen, who suffered endlessly as I wrote this and truthfully answered the question "Is that funny?" about 5,000 times.

Ian, Erin, and Ali, for baby-sitting, laughing, and wearing all the knitted stuff.

My darling Joe and my daughters Amanda, Megan, and Samantha, for never getting sick of it all, for thinking that the book was cool, and for eating a lot of pizza toward the end.

Finally, I need to thank every knitter that I ever met. This book is about you.